PRAISE FOR
A PATH OUT OF EXILE

"After coming to post-war Paris, Grunwald's meeting with Gurdjieff marked the turning point in his search for genuine freedom. The stunning account of a life in contact with a real master provides an intimate picture of the Work in its gathering momentum. A must read."
—DAVID APPELBAUM, author of *Voice* (SUNY Press)

"'*His large black eyes with their extraordinary expression seemed to be questioning me...They revealed a serenity from which radiated intense affliction, a sort of sacred sorrow, along with an ironic malice....*'
"So runs the startling description by François Grunwald of his first encounter with G.I. Gurdjieff. One notes similar unexpected insights and a steady dedication to truth throughout as Grunwald transports readers into the turbulent France of last century, illuminating not only Gurdjieff and his Work but other notables including Mme. de Salzmann and Henriette Lannes.
"This may be the final memoir ever published of working with Gurdjieff. It is an essential addition to that invaluable genre, a worthy read for all those seriously interested in the man and his teaching."
—JEFF ZALESKI, Editor and Publisher, *Parabola*

"More than compelling, Grunwald's story touches the miraculous. It's profoundly encouraging, and a priceless addition to the Gurdjieff literature."
—RICHARD WHITTAKER, Founding Editor and Publisher, *works & conversations* Magazine

A PATH OUT OF EXILE

With Gurdjieff in Post-war Paris

FRANÇOIS GRUNWALD

Translated by
THIERRY GUILLEMIN and
ANNE SULLIVAN

Foreword by
ROGER LIPSEY

Red Elixir
Rhinebeck, New York

A Path Out of Exile: With Gurdjieff in Post-war Paris Copyright © 2025 by Thierry Guillemin and Anne Sullivan

All rights reserved. No part of this book may be used or reproduced in any manner without the consent of the publisher, except in critical articles or reviews. Contact the publisher for information.

Paperback ISBN 9781966293101
eBook ISBN 9781966293118

Library of Congress Control Number 2025908250

Red Elixir is an imprint of Monkfish Book Publishing Company

Red Elixir
22 East Market Street, Suite 304
Rhinebeck, New York 12572
(845) 876-4861
redelixirbooks.com
monkfishpublishing.com

TRANSLATORS' ACKNOWLEDGMENTS

We wish to thank the family of François Grunwald, especially his daughter Francine, for the care they have taken with the original manuscript and their permission to include here the previously unpublished family photographs of their father for the cover. At *Éditions L'Originel*, publisher of the French edition, Jonas Endres and Claire Mercier responded with kindness in permitting publication of Part III in English. This edition owes much to the expertise of Paul Cohen as publisher and editorial adviser and Colin Rolfe as designer at Monkfish. To Barbara Probst we owe a debt for her meticulous final review of our translation. Roger Lipsey, who contributed the introduction, happens to have been in Paris for the launch of Dr. Grunwald's book and immediately recognized that key pages should find their way into English.

It has been our joy to accompany François Grunwald on his path out of exile.

Thierry Guillemin and Anne Sullivan

Contents

Foreword by Roger Lipsey   vii

I	Return to Savoie	1
II	Distraught and Aimless in Paris	12
III	Reunion with My Brother and Ludolf Schild	22
IV	Landholder and Arborist in Chinon	27
V	Inner Spaces Open Up	40
VI	In the Group of Mme. H.	49
VII	Meeting with Gurdjieff	61
VIII	The Circle of Idiots	69
IX	A Double Life	80
X	The Fourth Way	94
XI	In Memory of…	103
XII	1948 — Paris or Chinon?	114
XIII	1949 — A Capital Year	129
XIV	Death of Ludolf	137
XV	You! — *Deutscher Oberlokomotifconduktor*	148
XVI	The Last Days — The Death of Mister Gurdjieff	159
XVII	Toward Something Else — Exile Is Also a Mourning	169

Afterword by Francine Grunwald   175

FOREWORD

"Earth, not safe place!" So said Gurdjieff one morning at the Turkish bath in Paris, in the company of François Grunwald and other men of his circle. Grunwald and Gurdjieff were doing a somewhat ritual inventory of their scars: Grunwald's acquired in World War II, fighting northward in Italy with the Free French Forces, Gurdjieff's acquired in a long life often in risky places in early years. This book is a memoir and autobiography, likely the last eyewitness account we shall have of life with Gurdjieff and his closest pupils, and one of the most insightful. Its publication in French in 2017 was a complete surprise; a memoir literature that had long since seemed exhausted — who else could write, so many years after Gurdjieff's passing in 1949? — was suddenly alive with memory, with freshness. Completed in 1987, it waited thirty years "in the drawer" for the perfect publisher. To my mind, it is a masterpiece, however little currently known or recognized. In this introduction I want particularly to evoke the earlier years of Grunwald's life before he met Gurdjieff.

Is the idea of a *Bildungsroman* familiar to you? For Grunwald, born and raised in Vienna, choosing exile just months after the Nazi Anschluss of 1938 that converted Austria into a somewhat willing province of "Greater Germany," the idea of the *Bildungsroman* was infinitely familiar. Goethe and other classic authors whom he knew well had created the model. *Bildung* can be translated as education, but it has wider and deeper connotations touching on the acquisition, slowly, through crisis and reflection, of a mature, effective human identity. The scale of many such novels is somewhat intimate: the learning gets done, as in Thomas Mann's *Magic Mountain*, among a relatively small number of protagonists and typically without violence. Not so for Grunwald. The landscape of this autobiography, after a carefree boyhood in Vienna roaming the city, roaming knowledge, is the horror of mid-twentieth-century Europe. Grunwald's educator was what Gurdjieff called "the terror of the situation" in acute form: oppression, exile, loss, war, near-fatal injury. He learned ten thousand things, and in the end found his way to what he had instinctively wished from quite early years. Then his education continued on another basis.

Grunwald was born in 1917 in Vienna to a reasonably prosperous, culturally advanced family of assimilated Jews. His father was a patron and friend of leading artists, including the permanently outrageous, brilliant painter Egon Schiele and others in the Vienna Secession movement. A Schiele portrait (1917) of his father Karl Grünwald now hangs — how objects travel — in a Japanese museum. One of the best ways to understand a crucial time and place is to follow the experience of just one person, vividly narrated with a strong sense of context. This is precisely what Grunwald offers as Austria flowers culturally after World War I and gradually falls under the shadow of Hitler's Reich. The earlier pages are something like a love letter to pre-Anschluss Austria, despite the growing pressure even on schoolchildren of anti-Semitism. "Still today," he writes in 1987, "I remain saturated in one way or another with the universal character of this city, or better, this place of culture."

But it was unkind to him and to all Jews, however much they had enriched the city with literature, art, music, commerce, civic responsibility, and, not least, the birth and elaboration of a new way of looking deeply into human nature — psychoanalysis. The Anschluss in March 1938 — Grunwald was just 21 years old, ambitious to begin medical study — inaugurated a time when he sensed what was to come. "I not only intuited in advance the extermination of the Jews, I knew it in advance, and with certainty. Unfortunately, I was incapable of transmitting this conviction, which I experienced almost physically, to my poor unconscious mother and sister; words were wholly unable to capture these inner processes." Grunwald knew that he would emigrate; it was only a question of when, and the rest of the family understood as much: parents, brother, sisters. They would all find their way out by different routes, although — as the last words of this book record — his mother and one of his sisters, imagining themselves safe in southern France, were deported and murdered in Auschwitz.

The family apartment overlooked the wide avenue where Hitler made his triumphant entry into Vienna; the family looked out on this unforgotten scene from their windows. Grunwald was beginning to prepare his departure. "I stayed three months longer in Vienna, but inwardly I had already left." The last insult for him personally occurred when young Nazi thugs ambushed, humiliated, and beat him mercilessly. He had options to consider. An expert skier who had earned money, to his great pleasure, as a ski monitor in the Alps, he could have skied to Switzerland clandestinely and somehow found his way on. He chose instead, on good advice, to obtain a passport — still possible for a short time, then impossible — and take the train through Germany, where he discovered on the train and during a few improvised days in Berlin that there was less overt anti-Semitism at that time among ordinary people than in his homeland. His onward passage was straight out of fiction, though true: imagine a young Jewish man with "J" stamped on his Austrian passport who had to reapply, successfully, for a "Greater Germany" passport at the Gestapo office in Berlin. In time he safely reached Paris, where an uncle received him. War had not yet come, but he knew that war was coming, he intended to fight that war, not with hatred toward the German people — he states this often — but to do all he could as an individual to free Europe from the hateful regime he had left behind. "A chapter of my life, youth, had ended. I experienced the beginning of something else."

Striking, as this story progresses, is that we are hearing from a man of long years who looks back with what seems total recall on the young man he was. There is wisdom in his words, even in chapters where he narrates what amounts to a war story as gripping as the best in the genre. That wisdom isn't detachment; he is fully engaged as a storyteller. It is an intelligence, a kind of aeration or atmosphere that allows each event and moment to be seen and felt. Alongside the outer landscape of prison, danger, total war, friendships and brutal losses, there was an inner landscape to which he introduces us. "I entered gradually into a quite singular inner state that increased during my departure from Germany. Everything was taking place as if I was guided, nearly directed in my actions and initiatives. By what? By whom? 'Something other'? If so, what? It was at the riskiest, roughest moments of this journey that I felt most concretely guided, securely and prudently. I only had to execute, attentive to a certain tension in me which, when it became too strong, swallowed up my energy and stripped me of that strange teleguidance. Where did it come from? Maybe the gods know, I don't, although its existence was beyond any possible doubt. Later, during the war, I experienced this same state with still more intensity."

In those first years in France before war broke out, he found his way. He even met and became engaged to the daughter of a prosperous, entrepreneurial family of bakers, trained and then worked in a small creamery in Normandy, making butter and cheese. However, when war came in 1940, he was interned by the French police as a citizen of "Greater Germany." That wasn't to last long: a decree offered young men in his category, many of them émigré Jews, the opportunity to serve in the French Foreign Legion. He jumped at the opportunity. Given a three-day leave by the military authorities to which he now reported, he and Denise married and feted their wedding with her parents at a chic restaurant before he was obliged to leave, just days later, for Morocco to train as a Legionnaire.

"Living with such a band of brigands had its interest. How many stories I heard of crimes, fights or escapes spilled out by men who were seriously drunk. Yet an iron discipline prevailed. . . . The new recruits, engaged 'for the duration of the war,' volunteers . . . were two-thirds, like me, Jewish emigrants, the others political refugees from Germany and Austria." Despite his not unaffectionate mockery of the Legion, it was the scene of two most important changes in his life: he became a trained warrior, and he met Ludolf Schild. Half-Jewish, German, originally from Hamburg, Schild had settled in Paris in 1936 to pursue his education and career as a dancer and choreographer. He had found his way to the Legion just as Grunwald had: it was an available, rough shelter, offering a way to fight the war. His wife Nadia followed him to Morocco and makes occasional appearances at the Legionnaires' camp.

Here is yet another moment in Grunwald's life that seems covered with light. Exceptionally handsome, a strong and gifted dancer who fought and prevailed in single combat with the few "brigands" who dared to test him, Schild became Grunwald's inseparable friend. "His spiritual evolution had already carried him very far," writes Grunwald, "and I looked up to him with eyes of gratitude. I sensed that his level of being was obviously higher than mine, although out of modesty, one of his numerous qualities, he defended himself in that regard. . . I foresaw, I knew in myself, that Ludolph would guide me toward a higher spiritual orientation than I had any knowledge of. You can reproach me for playing the prophet after the fact, but I am certain that I sensed this already in the Legion." Schild was arrested by the Vichy French police on suspicion of being a spy after two excellent months of dialogue with Grunwald — despite the demands of life in the Legion, mostly in the cool of evening. Freed after heavy interrogations, his health affected and destined to die in his mid-thirties, Schild spent the war in Algiers teaching dance. The friends were richly fated to meet after the war.

The Vichy government demobilized from the Legion everyone who could find civilian work in North Africa or France. This became for Grunwald the occasion for two years of peaceful living in the French Alps, where Denise and her family had settled. A master skier and accustomed to working in the food industry, Grunwald found employment on the slopes and in a canning operation that packed snails at the right season, vegetables and meat at other times. This peaceful interlude changed invisibly in spring 1942, when Grunwald joined a Resistance group charged with storing arms and supplies in upland huts. Hard work, he was equal to it. It was at this time he first heard of the deportations to the east, to the death camps. "Then my attitude changed radically. If I had participated a little in the Resistance movement through a sense of justice and camaraderie, a taste for adventure, I was overcome with rage and definitively decided to fight."

It was fantastically difficult in collaborationist Vichy France to join a Free French combat unit. The best option was to find the way back to North Africa — through a dangerous trek, in part by night over the Pyrenees mountains, only to be met in Spain with a lengthy imprisonment under poor conditions, famished, and then on to a Spanish concentration camp (where conditions were a little better). The Franco government eased its treatment of young men hoping to join Free French combat units only when the fortunes of war began to turn and Franco sought friendlier relations with the Allied powers. During his time in what he calls the KZ, using German nomenclature for such camps, he received a message from a cousin in New York that an affidavit awaited him at the US embassy in Madrid, authorizing him to travel to America. He refused the offer. "It wasn't at all a question of heroism but of the very obvious duty to strive with all one's strength for the total elimination of the absolute, violent, and filthy calamity for the entire universe, this negation of humanity that was Hitlerism, be it at the price of my physical life. I acted without the least hatred for German soldiers."

Soon a delegation of French officers appeared in the KZ to solemnly announce that the way was clear for those who wished to join combat units in Morocco. Grunwald soon found himself in a predominantly Moroccan infantry unit destined for the fight to liberate Italy. He notes that the esprit de corps in his unit — comradeship, shared faith, shared readiness — differed entirely from what he had experienced in the Foreign Legion. The unit moved out to Naples and joined the war. Grunwald has the gift of narrating war; he brings you as close as the printed page can offer. The place names where he and his comrades fought figure in every history, especially Monte Cassino. Among other exploits he singlehandedly captured twelve German soldiers without a shot being fired, simply on the basis of his native knowledge of German and his shrewdness. His commanding officer was awarded the medal he deserved.

On what he calls a "terrible day," 12 May 1944, crouched for hours in a foxhole, he thought and thought. "I was thinking of my wife, of my son whom I knew so little, of my mother who had disappeared and my sister with her, filled with a sort of self-pity. There was no direct fear, but a pervasive feeling penetrated my entire being with regret. I still wished to live many things more important than just simple, organic life, and I mourned in advance this enormous loss, the lack of what life promised me. An immeasurable sadness filled me, leaving me infinitely sad and moved, in an inner region of being that I had never before entered, and in the end, I prayed to be granted to live. . . . So it was that during those ten hours which often obsessed me later, a new knowledge entered me, introduced as if by a pneumatic hammer." This is Grunwald at war: a resourceful and courageous warrior, a man of keenest sensibility.

He was seriously wounded on the 22nd of May during the advance to a place called Pontecorvo. Thrown into the air by an exploding artillery shell, he was temporarily blinded and, as his comrades later told him, moaning. He was carried to a front-line hospital, his body filled with shrapnel, one of his hands permanently damaged. He would need a year to recover — like all his years, brilliantly and meticulously recounted. As a wounded veteran, he was granted French citizenship in five days — not much paperwork for such as him.

The last scene we need to know before this book takes us further is an oceanside café in Rabat where Grunwald reflects back through his experience. "In an unclear way, I felt like a marionette, a puppet, whose strings had been guided in some mysterious way until now. I drifted for years in a torrential river where, it's true, I had been able to swim, but the direction of its waters was given in advance." And he recalled his friend Ludolf, "toward whom I was drawn by affection mixed with veneration." They will meet again.

The complete book as published in French in 2017 under

the title *Un chemin hors de l'exil: De Freud à Gurdjieff*, is in three parts. This book you have in hand is the third and final part, translated into English, telling the story of the post-war years in France. As you will see, it is addressed to a friend, Richard Dill, as if it were a continuous letter. In pages to come, Grunwald will tell us what he means by exile: not just exile from Austria, though that remains unforgotten. There was for him another exile, a longing for home not defined by place but by an identity understood, earned, deepened, set in motion for the good. The path out of exile leads there, and Grunwald — expert skier, mountain guide — found the guides he needed.

Roger Lipsey

Chapter I
RETURN TO SAVOIE

I was returning to France on a ship of expatriates, traveling across the Mediterranean from Algiers to Marseille in November of 1944.

A telegram had been sent from Algiers to the former gendarmerie major Ménard, now Lieutenant-colonel Ménard, who was waiting for me on the dock. The Vichy government had promoted him, and it would be useful for him to be seen with an immigrant, a wounded war veteran like me. Everything goes full circle in this world! Previously, for an immigrant to know a gendarme was something very advantageous. Now that the Germans were retreating, an immigrant became a valuable connection for a lieutenant-colonel of the gendarmerie.

In the Vienna of yesteryear, it was said of a man who led a pleasant and good life: "He lives like God in France!" Where and how did this curious saying originate? What does it mean? What wisdom is hidden there?

In a superficial way, it speaks to that pleasant art attributed to the French of enjoying exquisite delicacies, fine wines and ravishing women. But these are the pleasures of a king, rather than of God. "Living like God in France" does not concern tourists or temporary residents who are foreign to the country but rather speaks to a deep, intimate and mysterious familiarity, such an ease that God himself might feel.

Certainly this intimacy with France does not come so easily. Rather, a passing traveler feels the inconvenience of manifest xenophobia, at least at first. But when the ease of being shows itself beyond appearances, one finds in the French an essential interior freedom towards themselves and others. Whoever has carefully listened to or read the impartial and rigorous observer G. I. Gurdjieff understands this. The chapter *"France"* in his *Beelzebub's Tales to his Grandson* offers many striking contributions to this subject.

Rejected, expelled and having felt that xenophobia painfully even in France, I returned as a wounded and mutilated "hero," confident that I would have no further internal or external difficulties. France had become my country. I had paid dearly for it, but now it was done. I was accepted. My naturalization for example was carried out in five days by the care of the military administration. A chief of staff, a relation of my wife's piano teacher, quickly moved my file forward, personally congratulating me on my "patriotic" attitude. "Becoming a French citizen usually takes three years," he told me, "but I put your file above the others."

No more difficulties or hassles for papers or residence permits! Only those who have experienced these things appreciate what a waste of time a stateless person must suffer, what degrees of anguish he must go through. But a foreigner who is more or less well received knows how uniquely off-putting the "Office for Foreigners of the Prefecture of Paris" can be. Not that anyone was ever tortured or cruelly treated there. No, the torments are more refined: waiting, waiting for hours and days in premises that are too cramped, being sent from one desk to another, from one official to another very far away, still waiting to hear finally: "Come back tomorrow!"

There I was. It was over once and for all. I was removed from the list of wanderers.

I had been thinking of these things, while sailing the Mediterranean. Until the age of sixteen or seventeen, I had led an uncomplicated life without much worry, protected by the concrete walls of a benevolent ignorance. It formed a cage, a shelter of frivolity and carelessness, though sometimes pierced by certain athletic ambitions where the weight of existence was not revealed. Dramas and tragedies that took place only in the theater and novels allowed a taste of these imaginary and artistic excitements — and then I would return to the pleasant comfort of ignorance. I preferred stupidly simple jokes and skits to anything else. I loved entertaining absurdities and the laughter that arose when obvious contradictions or incongruities emerged. I still have several suitcases full of such jokes.

Then just before my seventeenth birthday something happened, like an explosion, an unexpected event without any apparent reason or cause. My activity back then, or my inactivity, was to wait in vain for customers in my father's store. At six o'clock, after closing I would run to the large ice rink or to the city park to join my companions. We played, we laughed, we flirted, this latter occupation constantly accompanying all the others: ice hockey, skating, tennis…a carefree life with no shadows.

One afternoon while I was alone in the store standing between two shelves filled with fabrics, I was suddenly crushed. No roll of fabric fell on my shoulders, but an enormous inner pressure crushed me, squeezed me, without my having the slightest thought. I was not distressed but surprised by this strangeness, this weight, this extraordinary burden on my chest and my shoulders. I had to lean against the shelves of fabric, incapable of the slightest movement, and remain thus motionless for more than an hour. The strange thing is that no feeling, no thought could explain or mitigate this pressure. It touched a region of myself that was totally unknown. Even today, I have no rational explanation. It seems only that a monstrously heavy burden had been placed on my shoulders, and I could not bear it. Two hours later it was gone, and I did not worry about it, not having experienced it pathologically. But it remained vividly in my memory. I talk about it for the first time in this story, and I am far from having forgotten it fifty-four years later.

My carefree frivolity had been completely erased, and I had proof of it the next day. If I had at that time any religious or spiritual inclination, I would most likely have sought an interpretation of the phenomenon in this direction, but that was not the case. Something had been turned inside of me, and the engraved memory of that feeling of being crushed lingers, inextinguishable.

After that experience I had an irresistible impulse to read and learn, in a disorderly and wild way at first, then little by little, better structured. An irrepressible desire carried me wherever I could glean some knowledge and took me away from the places I had frequented before. To the questions of my comrades I answered with subterfuge, because in my former circle of friends, learning, reading or thinking was not very much valued. And then I was only a beginner and "every beginning is difficult," as the German proverb says, to which I can by countless lived examples testify to the truth.

Shortly afterward, I understood this inner event, but instinctively without formulating thoughts or words about it. Only being in action in the moment could make sense of this experience of strong compression, of oppression. It took me decades to express it in words: "You must give meaning to your life, a concrete meaning adapted to your abilities, not a general and vague meaning." I do not believe in the existence of a general meaning of life which would be the same for everyone, except perhaps a very high meaning that few men can reach and only with the help of grace.

Thus, after some reflection and hesitation, the decision to become a doctor took hold of me. It persisted and remained alive, though it had to yield temporarily during the dangerous times of emigration, persecution and war, which relegated that possibility to the future.

When one finds himself in danger of losing his life, that is to say in danger of death, it is the present that matters — more precisely, presence of mind and a sense of personal agency. Everything depends on survival, but not at any price. If we want to give meaning to this life, then we must be able to look at ourselves in the mirror without shame. In life, fate plays a demanding game with everyone. This results in feelings of guilt which if not understood, or falsely atoned for, can lead to bewilderment. There are genuine feelings of guilt which painfully point to a true path. Unfortunately, there are also false or futile guilt feelings that engender psychological confusion. The latter belong to the realm of psychotherapy, a field in which I have much experience both as an affected victim and as a doctor of the soul.

As a wounded soldier looking into the distance up to the heights of the ancient port city of Marseille and its Christian monument, *Notre-Dame de la Garde,* I saw myself as a cripple. I limped visibly. I needed two canes to walk and had only one hand to hold them adequately. I called myself a "cripple," unaware that this designation, experienced as a condemnation, was a huge miscarriage of justice. I was wounded internally, psychologically. I had a gaping wounded soul. I did not know that a severe prosecutor dwelling in myself had arrived at this decision without any defense lawyer being present during the process. The next two years were marked by an unconscious shift from the psychic realm to that of the soul, the inner self, accompanied by sad and senseless conflicts with myself and with others and an inability to decide anything whatsoever on my own.

One day, Richard, you confronted me roughly in Munich. It was on Poschingerstrasse, at the bottom of the Herzog Park: "Tell me clearly and simply once and for all, what is this 'unconscious' that everyone is talking about without having any clue! It's crazy drivel, damn it!"

I did not know what you had picked up by chance on this subject from various amateur psychological groups — a subject, as I pointed out to you, that I had never mentioned in my discussions and somewhat abstract explanations. As you listened to my response, you quickly became mentally absent. Praise be to God, because two words are enough to say it all: "active" and "unknown." Something unknown to us is constantly and actively at work in our inner life. It was Arnaud Desjardins who introduced me to this exhaustive, albeit very brief, explanation.

A man does not yell at his wife merely because the coffee is cold, and a woman does not sulk at her husband merely because he comes home late! These are very simple examples of neurotic states. One could also find positive forms of expression although they are rarer. General usage makes "neurotic" an ignominious qualifier, a very pejorative word. It is however the serious suffering of the soul in the sinister thorny thicket of life.

Thus totally ignorant of my true state, I was cordially welcomed upon disembarking on the dock by Lieutenant-colonel Ménard. Nobody checked those who were landing, which surprised even a gendarmerie officer. An on-duty gendarme took my luggage and drove us in a service car to the apartment where Madame la Colonel was waiting for us.

M. and Mme. Ménard — may they rest in peace — told me about events from the time of German occupation and the liberation which had occurred only three months before. Ménard, a senior officer, faced many difficulties. The gendarmerie did not want to recognize his promotion to the rank of lieutenant-colonel which had been awarded by the Vichy government. Fortunately his troubles seemed to be easing, thanks to the intervention of his cousin, a major general and freemason.

But now they wanted to transfer him to the north of France after he had been living on the shores of the Mediterranean for twenty-five years. What grief, which brought tears to Madame: "There is so little sun there."

Ménard mentioned he might need a paper from me attesting that he had always been an enemy of the Germans and always had philosemitic convictions. As courteously as I could, I promised him this certificate, knowing full well that he had never been either for or against the Germans and that his career and his wife constituted the full extent of his existence. This paper turned out to be unnecessary, since the freemason and major-general cousin proved to be enough. Yet was it not flattering that a Jewish corporal could provide cover for a Catholic lieutenant-colonel with his recommendation?

I learned from Ménard and others how unjustly and cruelly the spontaneous fighters of the resistance had often behaved, especially those who rallied at the last moment. New vigilantes, they carried out acts of personal revenge under the guise of reprisal. Many men were executed and imprisoned without any real investigation or trial. This is how the pressure of the

German occupation exploded after the liberation, and these surges of hatred were still taking place while we were discussing it in Marseille.

I did not witness any scene of this kind, but almost a year later I had to provide certificates for my previous employer at a dairy and cheese factory in Normandy, the Swiss captain Rutz. He and his wife had been detained by resistance fighters in appalling conditions. Obviously he had delivered butter and cheese to the Germans and with their help requisitioned all the milk in the region. After the liberation the resistance fighters threatened him with death for weeks and held him for six months before transferring him to the official justice system.

According to Schiller: "It is the curse of all wrongs that they must perpetuate themselves, always engendering other evils."

I add: "It is the blessing of any genuine good deed that it must inevitably lead to oneself."

Despite having great interest in politics before the war, I had none afterward. It was only in 1958, having completed my medical studies, including a specialization in psychiatry, that the impact of de Gaulle returning to power in France reawakened this interest in me. De Gaulle as a politician was exceptional, unique.

I stayed a day and a half with M. and Mme. Ménard without the ability to contact my wife in Savoie. Nothing functioned then in France, not telegrams, nor scarcely any other official business. The trains ran more poetically than efficiently. Many bridges had been destroyed. Every corner of the trains was crowded, even the toilets. Two train employees freed up for me with difficulty a place at the window reserved for the wounded. As a wounded soldier with medals, I was kindly received.

Trains have always been my favorite mode of transport. I appreciate pleasant train trips, and this long and tiring journey from Marseille to Chambery was full of friendly encounters in spite of the constant detours and compartments packed with travelers. Conviviality happens quickly in a train compartment, compared to what happens on a plane or bus. One comments on the events of the day and one is not embarrassed to express worries or complaints. Go across India by train, Richard, and you will learn more in three days than you would in three months in planes and hotels.

Conversations in our compartment centered primarily around the catastrophic food situation. From 1944 to 1948 France was hungry. The black market was flourishing and the passengers were very interested in exchanging information about prices. One man probably wanting the good opinion of his companions and confident in his superiority, smiled and offered chocolate and cookies to everyone: "First of all, for the soldier," he said. And he asked me to relate something about the war.

Aided by the chocolate which was a real treat, I spoke about my escape through Spain along with several anecdotes of the war. I recall one woman who made the same remark at least twenty times during the hour: "Oh! Won't your wife be happy!"

People from the south of France are specialists in emotional concern for one another, whether positive or negative. In one corner a young woman was weeping in a restrained way. She had no news of her husband or her brother. It was explained to her that the prisoners and deportees were being kept in Germany but she would see them return since the end of the war was near. She calmed down.

The train stopped often and for long periods — a good thing because going to the toilet was difficult enough at the stops and impossible along the way. From Marseille it took twenty-four hours to reach the destination of Chambery, *préfecture* of Savoie. I was going to Moutiers, seventy kilometers farther in the mountains. "There is no train, I was told. It comes maybe every two or three days but it is very uncertain."

Nevertheless, a military vehicle picked me up immediately in front of the station. Each day three or four soldiers made the run between Chambery and Bourg-St-Maurice near the Italian border. They reported that "Battles still continue above Bourg-St-Maurice. The Germans are retrenched beyond the Petit Saint-Bernard pass. There are many artillery shots but no troop movement and hardly a single loss."

The soldiers took me to my house next to the cathedral of

Moutiers, and I hobbled up the two flights. My wife Denise opened the door. Tears, silence, then hugs and kisses. Soon we began to speak more freely as the sun set behind the cathedral, brightening our reunion. I found Denise unchanged. She spoke right away of our son Jean-Pierre who was already asleep. We knew about our respective adventures from our letters to each other. In fact she had received one of my letters from Algiers that very morning, telling of my hope to return soon.

Then she awakened our little boy, now aged two and a half. He slowly stood up on his bed, rubbing his eyes and looking at this stranger in uniform whom his mother held around the waist. His look darkened and he began to cry.

"It is papa. It is papa," she said several times.

But the little gentleman jumped from the bed and huddled against his mother, instinctively understanding that the exclusive possession of her was over, and from now on he would have to share her with this stranger, which did not suit him at all. I took him on my lap and slowly his fear subsided.

Jean-Pierre was tall for his age and spoke well, forming complete sentences. The next day his reticence disappeared, though he often tried to claim sole possession of his mother.

We came to a day at the end of November 1944 when it had snowed during the night and the weather was cold and sunny. I set out with my family across the small town, walking slowly along the narrow road that led uphill to the big ski slope, often welcomed, stopped, and asked to speak. From there one could see in the distance the high mountains shine brightly under the sun. I had previously exercised there in the winter. But now I had much difficulty on the snowy and slippery paths and my two canes barely sufficed. The view of the mountains and the snow darkened my mood bit by bit.

It is over for me now, I repeated to myself. The mountain had been one of my reasons for living. I had an inner relationship with it especially in winter, and now this relationship was going to disappear. This renunciation imposed by my physical wounds brought in its wake other, less natural, renunciations imposed by my ignorance.

The husband, the returning father, changed into a gloomy cripple in whom frustrations worked their way to destruction. The powerlessness of my wounded legs in this glowing ski area became overwhelming. I became an irritable, bothersome walking companion. Our little boy began to cry and my irritation grew. Our walk ended. I made the irrevocable decision to leave the town of Moutiers and the mountains as quickly as possible.

I dragged around sadly for the fifteen days that followed, preparing our departure for Paris with repressed frustrations about skiing and the mountain. Nevertheless I found friends and acquaintances of whom some were true resistance fighters. I say "true" because in Savoie as elsewhere relatively few men joined the resistance before the last moment and took up arms before the departure of the Germans. In any case there would not have been enough weapons for all of the volunteers.

The German retreat through the valleys of the Alps toward Italy was accompanied by horrible cruelties. The resistance fighters attacked the exhausted troops in the mountains and the Germans took frightful revenge on the civilian population.

The intervention of the former mayor of Moutiers, Marius C., was courageous. The resistance, he told me, had occupied Moutiers and taken as prisoners twenty German officers and soldiers who were staying there. Several battalions of German mountain fighters could be seen arriving from a distance, rushing down the steep slopes of the mountains. The French resistance rapidly pulled back in the face of the German superiority in equipment and troops, and the Germans captured all the men of Moutiers who were not hiding. Mayor C. tried to negotiate with the Germans. At first he was harshly refused; then later he was better received by a captain whom he described as very reasonable. This German captain revealed during a one-to-one discussion that he was nervous about several of the S.S. officers and was waiting for them to leave before liberating the men. This was done with the exception of twenty to thirty people whom he held hostage. Other troops arrived and the resistance fighters returned considerably reinforced, igniting an intense and wild battle.

These days of the war produced a hero I came to know well: the barber of whom I was a regular client. In a very reckless way and motivating all the others, he took the lead of a group that stormed the German officers' headquarters, taking all the Germans prisoner and saving Moutiers from a perilous situation. The next day he opened his shop, growling and refusing the celebration honoring him. He wanted nothing to do with that.

He received me kindly when I visited him and animated his story with invectives and insults in a tasty Savoyard slang of such vulgarity that I cannot repeat: "These assholes strut around now with officers' stripes freshly made by their good wives and medals which they have invented. The accountant, this big mouth, you know him. He does not even know the difference between a colonel and a major. All of this disgusts me. Where were our weapons? Do you know? Of course below near Albertville, being parachuted. And who has caught them? The communists! They organized this! Just wait and see what happens now that they are armed. I cut hair, I shave and I dress hair, and they can kiss my ass or forget about me, it's all the same!"

The expressions of this man were actually even harsher, and I found his attitude an example worthy of following. I had heard plenty of stories of the resistance and the vengeance on the part of the Germans as well as the French, so I had my fill of it and all the politics after the battles. I, myself, could also tell many stories from North Africa and Italy where politics, cowardice and career ambitions played principal roles. But why stir the stinky excrement and spread nauseous odors? There was at that time a struggle for power in France between the well-armed communists and the Gaullist nationalists. The challenge was considerable but the Marshall Plan and American economic aid tipped the scale to de Gaulle's advantage.

As I have already told you, for many years I was not interested in politics. But I cannot say what interested me then, upon my arrival in Paris at the end of November 1944 with wife, child and mother-in-law, after a long and difficult trip by train.

Chapter II
DISTRAUGHT AND AIMLESS IN PARIS

The fourteen months following my arrival in Paris at the end of November 1944 were the darkest of my life. I see them today as a long journey toward "the mount of purification," through a tunnel as dark as a night in purgatory.

This black abyss had been carved into my innermost self. It had to do with the state of my soul. Outside, on the contrary, I was swimming in unsurpassable opulence. The incredible disparity between my inner state and my outer environment was unbearable. This was not an unexpressed psychological state of depression. A psychiatrist would likely put it in the category of psychotic separation, a kind of fragmentation. Risking one's life in war requires a certain level of courage and the willingness to sacrifice, but no special knowledge. On the other hand, finding one's personal ethic is quite different and requires, if one does not want to fail, a very high level of understanding.

This interior state did not affect my intellectual and emotional relations with those around me. It touched me on a deeper level, which one could call existential. I no longer saw any meaning anywhere and I suffered greatly. At the same time, this suffering — so terribly present and of such incredible intensity — seemed senseless. On the surface I behaved normally, like foam on the water. To call this state "depression" would be wrong, as there was never the slightest thought of self-destruction, which would have been the height of absurdity. The essence, my central core, had already collapsed. Destroying my corporeal life made absolutely no sense.

I considered all sorts of professions available to a man who was a father, since my wife was expecting a second child. I looked for professional courses. I visited schools to take a look. I gathered information everywhere, especially in the offices of the university, and everywhere I was confronted with the feeling that it was meaningless because of my total disinterest. I could not tell anyone about it because I did not understand it myself. What the hell can we understand from the bottom of a black hole? If I refer to this period of time as a passage through the purification mount of purgatory, it is not from hyperbole or pretentious bombast. Such states from a psychiatric viewpoint would drive one to madness. But as one of my most experienced professors of psychiatry once pointed out very distinctly: "Not everyone who wants to go crazy can do so. It takes a lot of talent."

I would like to convince you, Richard, so you can understand what follows, that while experiencing the things I am trying to describe here, I was totally unaware of them. I also want to make it very clear that no one caused this state of suffering. No one was responsible for it, neither my wife, nor my parents-in-law, nor even social or family circumstances. There were obviously conflicts more or less repressed in me with my close entourage. But Monsieur de La Palisse[1] would say that the conflicts can arise only with someone who happens to be there! This dear La Palisse is too often forgotten both by those involved in conflicts and in the psychological theories that explain them; the result is many guilt feelings toward a father or mother or others.

The existential drama that agitated me was expressed essentially by my gloomy attitude. Added to this I had constant nightmares of war that persisted for several years. Most were extremely violent fantasies, visions of bloody combat that made me scream at night, frightening and waking up the quiet sleepers around me.

In my public life I had very limited occasion to meet with old

---

[1] Jacques de la Palisse (1470-1525) was a French nobleman whose epitaph "*s'il n'était pas mort il ferait encore envie*" was slightly misread and became appreciated as a pun "if he were not dead, he would still be alive." Since then, an expression to denote an utterly obvious truth is called in French a *Lapalissade*.

friends, former army comrades, government or hospital employees. People I encountered in the street or the metro lived quite sparingly, if not in misery, almost without money, and were often cold and hungry. On the other hand, at home I was in a veritable land of plenty, awash in an opulence I had never known before. We sat down every day, noon and evening, at a well-stocked table for long lavish meals to which my in-laws often invited acquaintances who were eager to be truly satiated for once.

My parents-in-law were well-to-do people and had been so even before the war. Their talent for business, together with their reputation for honesty and seriousness, had earned them esteem in the circles of grocers and in particular with their peers: bakers and pastry chefs. My mother-in-law had a remarkably entrepreneurial spirit. She feared neither God nor the devil nor her husband, who never opened his mouth unnecessarily. This couple complemented each other effectively in all business ventures. While Mme. Bretonnière took bold initiatives, M. Bretonnière maintained a steady ground with his silence, an icy silence that everyone feared. The war had made them richer still, without any dishonesty I am sure.

In the circles of Parisian bakers and pastry chefs, commercial relations and exchanges were based on the kind of trust most often found in Asian cultures, without papers or justifications, without written contracts. Only the reputation of the old Bretonnière couple ensured their credit. They were sought out and lent money to start businesses. They were by no means coming from a patrician family and had worked hard to acquire their pre-war financial well-being. My father-in-law had started as a baker, and then my mother-in-law succeeded in transforming him from worker into the person in charge. Together they had acquired an unsurpassable, general common sense for commercial enterprises. One could have written a book about them such as *Debit and Credit* by Gustav Freytag, devoted to the history of a working-class family from the countryside and its gradual rise.

As a side effect, their human and social relations were completely in tune with their commercial affairs and financial status, from which came their value judgments. Of course personal conflicts easily ensued. With their daughter, my wife, and only with her, they had a pure, genuine and intimate emotional connection. Denise responded in the same simple way to their affection. She could have had everything, received everything, but in her modesty she almost never asked for anything. They showered her, no doubt, overwhelming her with unwanted things.

My wife's brother was much older than she was, a skillful libertine, generous with his friends, very shrewd in business, known throughout Paris for his debauched life. In contrast with Denise he had only business conversations with his parents. Mme. Bretonnière said of him: "He is the devil himself!" He too feared nothing and no one except his father and his mother from whom he hid all sorts of trickery and licentiousness. Discord resulted when public rumor reported these actions to them.

Mme. Bretonnière, a skillful and experienced businesswoman equipped with values in keeping with her abilities, obviously cared about the future of her daughter and wondered at the ever-so-strange attitude of her incomprehensible son-in-law. This one — yours truly, my dear friend — nested in this family like an outsider, a stranger to himself and to others except his wife. The problem was solved, and well solved for Denise by her deeply affectionate attitude toward me as well as toward her parents.

I am now convinced that anywhere else, in another family, and with other people, I would have felt just as much like an outsider. I had not fallen into the worst conditions, far from it. These people saw me as a necessary unavoidable burden. They knew of such situations and did not allow themselves to be disturbed or intimidated, as long as the table remained richly covered with the best dishes. Still, hanging around and letting myself live like this disgusted me.

Monsieur and Madame prepared these famously delicious and rich meals together skillfully despite their multiple obligations. They had the ingredients delivered from their many connections in Paris or the provinces. The table ritual followed a strict protocol: a punctual presence at 12:30 p.m. and again at 7:00 p.m. for the family meal which lasted about two hours.

Woe to the latecomer! A silent and icy look full of reproach from Monsieur punished any absence and any delay. Since then I dislike lingering at a table and prefer meals quickly dispatched. Any chatter that drags on after lunch or dinner arouses in me an aversion conditioned by these memories.

One of the reasons for human life here on earth is probably to acquire concrete experiences both positive and negative, that is to say pleasant and unpleasant. It wasn't until much later that I learned to appreciate unpleasant experiences in order to acquire true knowledge. Yet half of life if not more is made up of such painful or unpleasant experiences. We neglect them unconsciously. We refuse them, thus spontaneously discarding half of our vital energy — like wind blowing across the mountaintops and bypassing the valleys, height without depth, pleasure instead of knowledge. Like so many others I was trapped in a prison that my own opinions had shaped, blind to any way out.

In this very hospitable house, many guests were expansive in offering their worn-out opinions. I had to absorb all these *petit-bourgeois* points of view in endless chatter that could go on late into the afternoon. I had not much to say myself, yet was seized with a persistent feeling of disgust, which settled in me, for which I blamed myself and which I tried in vain to ward off.

I had to swallow while eating — with what sort of digestion you can only imagine — the anti-Semitic tirades where there always appeared a familiar and good "unique Jew," the "personally appreciated Jew" that everyone had in stock. It was not customary in front of this eternally taciturn head of the family to contradict his guests. Expressing Germanophile opinions was unforgivable especially when offered by those who had done so during the German Occupation. The slightest innocent remark like, "There are also good people among the Germans!" inevitably provoked frowns.

Learning that the soldier in front of them — I was only demobilized eight months later — disabled from war, in uniform with various medals, was an Austro-German Jew would have taken away the appetite of most of the guests! Even more, it would have shown a detestable lack of taste, since in all of Paris and in the whole of France hardly anyone had fought, perhaps one in a hundred. Maybe a little more if we consider as combatants the countless prisoners in Germany...

A soldier wounded at the front was a rarity as Germany still held a million-and-a-half prisoners. In the business circles I was in contact with, people did not think much of the real resistance fighters. When one did not have dirty hands, when one had not collaborated with the Germans, one really rejoiced at the liberation. But these liberators had only done their duty. Why did they have to stay in Paris? Yes, of course getting crippled in war is very honorable but if you think about it, it is pretty dumb and stupid, is it not? Which is not completely wrong.

My friend Sylvain — we had crossed the Pyrenees together — had joined General Leclerc and entered Paris in one of the very first tanks of his division. Then he was caught under German fire and found himself in mortal danger. During a visit with a few acquaintances he was considered a half-heroic, half-naive idiot: "And the worst thing," he told me sadly, "is that I really believe that I am."

Singularly, I was the only one at the table touched by these remarks which disgusted me. I mentioned it several times to my wife and always received the same answer accompanied by a look of reproach: "No one gives the slightest importance to this chatter. Shouldn't we also have fun at the table?"

I later learned that this cackling, which is like pouring from the empty into the void as the expression so aptly puts it, can be detrimental to our conservation of energy.

As a foreign creature installed in an existence of nonsense I had a thin skin. Vulnerable to everything that happened around me, I noticed everything, remembered everything. I had to accept that I would not be able to pursue my medical studies, exactly contrary to my wish and this gnawed at me. I was looking for a professional activity for the future and would repeatedly go to the Sorbonne to collect information from the office of the medical faculty. My Austrian baccalaureate allowed me to undertake any studies, and all careers were open to a naturalized French wounded combatant, all paths — except precisely one, that of medicine, for several reasons.

First, one could not begin medical studies without having a French baccalaureate. Second, a Vichy government decree that prohibited recently naturalized students from studying medicine was still in effect. Third, fourth, and strongest of all, I had condemned myself: I was a cripple, definitely incapable of becoming a fully practicing doctor. Finally and decisively, my mother-in-law pointed out to me very reasonably during a conversation that seven years of study would be far too long and far too expensive an investment. She did not know that in Paris no one exercises this profession without having received at least ten years of training. This was of course the main argument: my in-laws would have had to pay for my studies and at the same time provide for the maintenance of my whole family. Medicine was not well regarded in this environment. It was said, for example of a person who was a little eccentric, if he also read a number of books: "He works in medicine!"

If I had been a follower of astrology at that time I would have noticed with certainty that the sun and its procession of planets moved across the firmament in a particularly threatening way against my project of medical studies. I would have even observed that they did it intentionally for the sole purpose of being personally unpleasant to me. My own star, my main star located naturally well above the sun and its planets also appeared in a particularly hesitant way which was not helpful. And yet there was a small shooting star in the depths of myself which with hope slipped toward the other, the main star. However, it was too fragile to repel the negative stars and thus had no impact on the gloomy black hole of my inner dwelling.

I must in fact have been a strange fellow — am I still? My father-in-law himself, feared and respected by all, did not dare make me a serious professional offer. He entrusted that task to a person whose portrait I have already had the opportunity to paint.

Officer Ménard, now a colonel, came with his cousin General Stelle, a three-star division general, to try to help my brother-in-law out of considerable trouble due to a very imprudent generosity, the settlement of which had already been referred to the courts.

During a banquet-like dinner the general emphatically explained why joining this impudent resistance movement against the occupier had been impossible for him: "I would have been in constant danger of death!"

Is it not so, General, especially when life is all about shining in society? The danger is for others! As for the Ménard couple, the very corpulent Madame la Colonel had tears in her eyes, since she would soon have to follow her husband to Amiens: "It's the North Pole for me, but it's an unavoidable sacrifice!" she lamented.

Sacrifice necessary indeed for an appointment to the honor of colonel with five golden stripes. How could one have rotted miserably as a lieutenant-colonel?

My very energetic mother-in-law declared to the two senior officers in the middle of this memorable meal, in a dark and firm tone: "I ask you to help my son out of the pernicious mess he got himself into and if you do not, then all friendship is over between us."

A truly admirable attitude! It would have been hard to find anyone who knew better than she where she was heading.

It was after this eventful meal that the colonel took me aside and declared: "Your father-in-law would like you to work for him in his cinema."

To everyone's satisfaction, all the more manifest since it seemed to me that a refusal was expected, I accepted this solemn offer. The "Cité-Nord" cinema was just opposite the Gare du Nord, a stone's throw from the family apartment. The next day, I was checking the entrance tickets of the spectators before they descended into the screening room, which was located deep in a large cellar. During the absence of my father-in-law I could quietly read in the office. It had been agreed to grant me a few hours of freedom between 5:00 and 8:00 p.m. two or three times a week, depending on the need, so I could take courses and prepare myself for the profession of cinema controller. Then perhaps I could progress in rank. The director of the cinema who had been in charge of this function for several years was initially afraid of losing his job. But when he grasped my total lack of interest in advancement he became a friend or rather, a friendly accomplice.

M. Villiers, that was his name, was a typical Parisian, arrogant and shrewd, yet a good fellow, friendly, a sort of Beaumarchais's "Figaro" who could have been taken directly from the stage.[2] He was easy-going and quick-witted, always knew how to arrange everything, could provide anything to anyone and did not hesitate to do so, having friends both in the resistance and among the German collaborators. But his main skill was the art of matchmaking, finding each person his or her proper partner, according to their mutual desires and material compensation. No, he was not a pimp! It was out of pure cordiality — to please in an unselfish way his countless friends and girlfriends — that he arranged meetings. Being of service to the fellow citizens whom he liked had become a real addiction which required all sorts of relationships.

As for helping me resume my medical studies, that was the one thing he could not do. The stars were still against me. I had introduced him to my problem and he was truly upset by his lack of agency and mine. At the cinema he had personally chosen the six or seven ushers, really pleasant and pretty "ladies" who were elected to their position only by passing through the bed of the director. He had attached one of these ladies, a privileged one, to himself, and rented the others to friends or relatives to please them. He made it clear that thanking the usher with a gift or a jewel according to the fortune of the lucky man was welcome. Thus everyone was satisfied. Naturally, the son-in-law of the boss — and he feared this boss who was so eloquently taciturn — was excluded from these services. I had many other worries anyway.

My position in the family was then elevated by an important but quite intimate promotion: my father-in-law, to reward my acceptance of working at the cinema, invited me to use *tu* when

[2] The character of Figaro is a servant in several plays by Beaumarchais, including *Le Mariage de Figaro*.

addressing him. Monsieur Bretonnière used this familiar form with no one except his immediate family. I had therefore become a full member. On the other hand, I have addressed my mother-in-law as *vous* all her life, out of prudence on both sides.

Chapter III
REUNION WITH MY BROTHER AND LUDOLF SCHILD

My existence thus vacillated for a whole year from one side of the rue de Dunkerque to the other, from the apartment side to the cinema side. I have to say something about it in order not to be taken for a real zombie, which would be only relatively fair.

In the week from Christmas 1944 to New Year's Day 1945, the massive German offensive on Bastogne in Belgium caused great fear and concern in Paris and probably elsewhere too. The fear was followed and mitigated by the appearance of innumerable squadrons of bombers flying over Paris to Germany to drop their loads there. The final victory of the Allies was approaching and with it, festivities. The ushers in our cinema were terribly busy.

My brother Fritz had landed in Cherbourg in General Patton's army a month after the Allied landings of June 6, 1944. He was assigned to the second bureau of his regiment in the security department since he spoke German. As soon as Paris was liberated in August 1944 he visited my mother-in-law in her bakery and had already been to Paris twice before my arrival.

My brother and my mother-in-law were made for each other. A sympathy, an affection even — that I never managed to achieve — was established between them from the very first meeting. Frédéric, as my mother-in-law called him, was her *persona ultra grata*. For several reasons perhaps: first, he hardly spoke French, which prevented misunderstandings of language; then, he knew how to appreciate and esteem this extraordinary businesswoman; finally and mainly, my brother, unlike me, felt a deep hatred for the Germans. It was in him as an unconscious response to the deportation and murder of our mother and our sister. We did not have any confirmation of this fact at that time. We never received it, but we knew it intimately and with certainty.

Few French people could speak English — in particular very few senior officers — yet this American first-class soldier curiously was surrounded from his first visit to Paris by people fluent in the English language. He learned many stories and anecdotes of Parisian life under the Occupation. They told him about the quasi-heroic acts of my mother-in-law: how for example she had known how to keep her store open and constantly supplied for the Parisians, and how on several occasions she had thrown out German soldiers in uniform who came naively to buy some cakes, with insults as a bonus. The whole neighborhood knew about this purely emotional and very risky activity, this attitude of stubborn opposition which aroused in my brother a great respect for her. Her immediate family — her husband, daughter and son-in-law — did not know these things. We only learned about them later through my brother.

During the winter of 1944-45, when exactly I no longer know, a female voice told me in English on the telephone that my brother was at the American hospital in Le Vésinet, wounded, and was asking to see me. It was the first time I had seen Fritz since Vienna, and I found him lying in a hospital bed, vague, his eyes shining with a high fever. I was quite worried, since the wounds on his arm, hand and forehead were infected.

A few days later he was already much better. He told me about the fighting in the front near the Rhine where the Americans, bogged down and stuck in this location, resisted and took many losses.

He was on his feet quickly and paid us frequent visits before joining his regiment at the front two weeks later, taking part in the crossing of the Rhine towards the Palatinate. It was the final breach of the German front and the beginning of the end.

Fritz left me his PX cards and introduced me — since I was still in uniform — to the head of the American store in Paris. The PX was the distribution center of American goods for US soldiers staying in Paris. There I could get endless amounts of cigarettes that neither my father-in-law nor I smoked, chocolates, butter cookies, military shirts and pants, and hundreds of other things. Thus, not only did I have abundance and excess at home but I was also the recipient of the American super-superfluity, which I then distributed to others in Paris where everything was lacking at the time.

However, I was unmoved and took no interest in any of it. I was indifferent. For a bottle of whiskey I could have received a fortune which I did not need, and M. Villiers noted with anger my inability to do business. If only he had known what was really going on inside me! But how could he have known?

Fritz arrived one fine day in uniform in a Jeep filled to the brim, which we had to unload in the apartment, even stuffing various objects into the cellar and attic. He had come without written permission and left early the next morning after telling us the following story:

During the advance of the American regiments in the Palatinate, its security service was instructed to affix in each city, in each conquered place, posters on which were written in large letters the following orders:

EACH RESIDENT MUST IMMEDIATELY UNDER PENALTY OF SANCTIONS SURRENDER TO THE U.S. MILITARY AUTHORITY ALL WEAPONS AND EXPLOSIVES IN HIS POSSESSION.

I don't think my brother noticed anything about my inner state. His stays were brief and I felt better when he was there. He could also easily believe that my wounds were the cause of my strangeness.

Fritz had married Bobby in 1941. She had been between sixteen and eighteen when we first knew her, the only girl in our group of eight or ten teenage boys whom we took skiing and on mountain hikes, simply because she was the only female who could easily follow us. We called her "Bobby" so that we could tell our dirty stories in front of her. I was delighted when I learned they had married. They are still a close couple today.

At the end of 1945 my parents-in-law began to worry about my total lack of interest in the advancement of my position at the cinema and my gloom when I was there. The military hospital referred me to an internationally renowned hand specialist noted in particular for his skill in the meticulous surgery to repair the hands and fingers of people suffering work injuries. He performed three hours of subtle surgery under a large magnifying glass attempting to clean out and sew the tendons and sheaths of my left hand. When I woke up from the anesthesia, he came to my bed to explain to me: "We could certainly have completely restored your hand immediately after the injury, but this is very specialized surgical work that only seven or eight surgeons in the world know how to do. Who would have done it in a military general surgery hospital? I've tried everything, but your index and middle fingers will remain stiff. I tilted them a little. It will get better."

The army discharged me with a disability rating of forty-five percent. Later when I no longer felt so handicapped, the disability increased to sixty percent, and for the more than ten years that I've been almost unhindered I have been receiving eighty-five percent! This divergent and illogical development took place with the help of a lawyer specializing in these issues who followed the experts and always worked in anticipation of future aggravations.

A civilian now and disabled, what could I do with my life? My mother-in-law dreamed of owning a large property to grow fruit in the countryside, an estate with orchards. It was an old and persistent desire, strongly rooted in her. She often talked about it enthusiastically. She was probably tired of this gloomy son-in-law in her apartment too. I did try to find a separate place in Paris where I could study, but it was a rearguard fight and my project failed, especially because of the little energy with which I nourished it. At the beginning of 1946 therefore, we began to look in the countryside for a property with orchards.

It was then that my little star began to glow, the assembled heavenly bodies that had previously had such harmful effects loosened their embrace and a ray of light finally seeped into my black hole. This change was set in motion by a printed invitation I received for a dance performance by my comrade from the French Foreign Legion, Ludolf Schild. So he, he who understands me without words is now in Paris, I repeated to myself. Inner darkness comes from having forgotten the light. With this card, there entered a small but beneficial light.

The dance performance took place in a small hall far from our home, and when my wife and I entered Ludolf was already dancing. The stage was brightly lit and his noble face immediately attracted me again. A beneficent harmony emanated from him while he performed a series of solitary choreographies barefoot in various costumes or bare-chested. His wife Nadia, dressed in a low-cut black dress, accompanied him on the piano, but he himself conducted the music. I was as fascinated by the expressive and perfect dances as I was moved by the deep affection that was awakening in me.

Ludolf's conditions of living in Paris were very strenuous. He was giving dance lessons and was criticized for not earning enough money and therefore requiring his elderly mother-in-law to work in order to feed the family. In fact at the beginning of 1946, the inhabitants of Paris who were not privileged like we were led a very difficult life. He felt exhausted, almost sick and was both surprised and worried to experience such bouts of weakness. We talked for a long time recounting the events we had experienced since our separation. He was deeply disappointed, totally helpless and overwhelmed by the daily difficulties.

We saw each other a great deal during the two months I remained in Paris. I tried to help him as much as I could by bringing him money and various kinds of food. For the first time in Paris I realized that I needed money, because naturally, helping him had to remain secret. Talking about it at home would have caused me serious inconvenience. Several times, I attended silently the dance lessons he gave to a group of advanced students. I saw him come back to life with his class, regaining his fervor and sensitivity, but these moments were often followed by a state of great exhaustion.

Chapter IV

LANDHOLDER AND ARBORIST IN CHINON

A well-known real estate agency in Paris sent us a description several pages long of a large fruit-growing estate in Touraine. Mme. Bretonnière, overcome with delight upon reading it, immediately decided to visit this property. My mother-in-law's enthusiasm was easily explained but her haste had a particular reason.

This circumspect woman had been worried for some time, seeing her husband surround himself more or less in secret with certain shady bankers whom he invited to meetings in his office at the cinema. The meetings were of course reported in detail by the snitch M. Villiers. Mme. Bretonnière opened up without reservation to her daughter and to me. She had no confidence in this stock market business, knew nothing about it, understood nothing about it, and her husband understood even less.

"On no account do I want the family fortune to be squandered. I intend to save at least part of it for you," she said to her daughter.

She had learned that large money transfers would take place in the near future, so it was necessary to act quickly and she needed our help: "M. Bretonnière will not give in to my requests but he certainly will to those of his daughter," she declared.

We were, especially me, drawn to the totally unexpected, the new, the unknown. Thus the visit to the estate located near Chinon in Touraine, two hundred kilometers from Paris, soon took place. M. Bretonnière, a bit ill and unable to drive, miraculously agreed to lend his car, an almost sacred object of his attentive care, to his cinema director so he could drive Mme., her daughter and me to the estate.

It was grand, very grand! We had never imagined a residence of such sumptuousness and we stood open-mouthed, so impressed that we were unable to speak. Fifty-eight hectares surrounded entirely by high, thick stone walls, and trees as far as one could see, including sixty thousand apple trees. There were also two hectares of peach trees and two vineyards. Two wide and magnificent paths with tall evenly-spaced chestnut trees led to an imposing manor house, relatively recent but built, we were told, on the ruins of the old castle of Vaugaudry. At each end of the property stood a group of buildings, dwelling houses, barns, stables, cellars, cider presses and so on. There were, in a perfect state of preservation, the remains of a very old castle of exquisite harmony.

We hesitated, almost frightened in front of this large manor with wide marble staircases, immense living rooms on the ground floor and twenty bedrooms on the second and third floors, all quite richly furnished. The kitchen, also huge, was in the basement. M. Grandjean, an elderly professor of mathematics, was the owner. He received us with his young niece in the more than spacious dining room:

"My wife died six months ago," he told us. "It was she who used to run the entire estate but since the war and even a little before, since her illness, everything has been neglected. I don't want to stay here without her anymore, the memories are too painful for me. I want to leave quickly."

The problem for us was how to get used to living in such a sumptuous residence? The real estate agent and co-owner of the agency, a former cavalry officer appropriately noble and dressed to the nines, tried with all the persuasiveness he could muster from his familiarity with high society to convince us that it was not so difficult to get used to castle life. And indeed he succeeded by making the point, diplomatically, that all the fruit orchards would be sold at the "agricultural price" for the region because of their neglected state rather than at the "market price" for orchards and vineyards. On the other hand, we had to agree to keep for an affordable overall amount most of the furniture and paintings, except for certain items which would be negotiated.

The conversation was very animated in the car during our return trip. We were captivated by the charm and sumptuousness of this property, so it was now a matter of convincing the head of the family. Mme. Bretonnière advised her daughter to act alone since her father would not refuse her. Nothing was asked of me and nothing was necessary. This magnificent rural property, fallen from the sky, pushed my concerns and worries as if by magic, to the background.

M. Bretonnière's initial hesitation softened and then yielded under our enchanting descriptions, the skillful remarks of the cinema director about the possibilities of hunting and above all the tenderly imploring gaze of his daughter. The acquisition was promptly settled. The payment was made in gold coins which on the day of the settlement — with the inexplicable luck of the family business — were worth more than in the previous five years and more than they would be worth over the next ten years. A few days later the estate would have cost significantly more.

I attended all the ceremonies as a surprised spectator although I was, to tell the truth, an essential character, for it was up to me to manage this enterprise. Denise and I became co-owners of about twenty percent, and I agreed, according to the notarized settlement, to assume the position of unremovable responsible manager. The head of the family, hesitant at the beginning, later became more enthusiastic than anyone else, justifiably proud to own such a beautiful estate. He, the former baker.

For me it was another turnaround even more sudden and unexpected than the prior shifts. I had done nothing to make it happen, absolutely nothing. I had not even hoped for anything. It was a flash in a serene sky! An ironic astrologer might have commented that according to the concepts of licensed experts and recognized by all clairvoyants, my planets (mine, if you please) had just aligned in a beneficial way. And why would I not have directed them?

During the course of my life I have encountered men who have been pushed in all possible directions by their fate: some let themselves be seduced and became drug addicts; others let themselves be drawn by certain circumstances into crime and remained in prison for years. They had no innate disposition for that. They were simply pushed along. Some, because they did not know what to do, aimlessly pursued long academic studies. As for me, circumstances pushed me without the slightest intervention on my part, toward the possession of land, castles, wealth. This is how I became lord of the manor.

For a period of time I felt a certain inclination toward this new condition and threw myself body and soul into my new activity. I was only too eager to leave the enclosed environment of Paris with its musty atmosphere in which I lived, and in particular an apartment that was too cramped for all of us. Four months sufficed for the air of the country, the work in the orchards, and the total responsibility of the enterprise to improve my grim condition. The cane that helped me walk became less and less necessary. Soon I forgot it.

I spent my first weeks in Touraine with the math teacher M. Grandjean and his niece, learning the ins and outs of the property. M. Grandjean was from Geneva, a Swiss citizen, inventor of a method of shorthand known as "the Grandjean method" and used throughout the world. A friendly fellow, he delighted in long evenings after dinner when he would teach me all sorts of subtleties and mathematical intricacies mixed with humorous banter.

The manor also housed a large billiard room with a huge table, much larger than a typical billiard table. One evening M. Grandjean wanted to play. I pointed out to him that I hardly knew the game but he insisted that I join him. "You will see," he said, "that such a large table makes the game difficult even for good players."

By a happy coincidence my first shot perfectly hit the three balls. My second shot did so again and to top it off, my third too. It seemed to M. Grandjean both suspicious and funny. Had I been pretending? Had I concealed a great billiard experience from him? I had to defend myself and was able to prove my innocence because from that day on — not during the few weeks we spent together nor during the four years of my life as a landholder — did I manage such a feat again.

From April to July 1946 the entire estate was cleared and cleaned, especially the rows between the trees where the weeds had invaded everything. Almost half of the espaliered apple trees were dead or stunted and worthless. I hired a large number of agricultural workers from the surrounding area for this work and also for two months eight German prisoners of war. Most were from the eastern provinces of Germany, now Poland, where they were reluctant to return. Two of them worked for me for a year and then settled permanently in Touraine. One was called Dietrich, originally from East Prussia, now part of Russia. He was a relentless worker, very solid, who once told me: "A region so beautiful with such good wines. I have never seen one like this before."

Later he settled there with a winemaker ten kilometers from Chinon, and I sometimes ran into him in Touraine.

Our main activity was the care of the countless apple trees of different kinds and later the harvesting and sale of the apples. Secondarily there was the vineyard which we had to clear first like the rest of the property, followed by the harvest and vinification of the white wines.

We also made cider and large quantities of alcohol at the local distillery. In addition, it was necessary to take care of the hives — there were forty of them, sixteen of which were in operation — and to harvest the honey as well as tend a few fields of wheat and oats and a huge garden for everyone's vegetables.

Hunting was permitted all year round within the walls of the estate. When we had finished our work, the heavy tractors were rented to other farmers to pull the harvesters. We also had to cut down the trees in the forest, make firewood for everyone, and take care of the hay and straw for the horse. The fruit was eighty-five percent apples but at the beginning there were peaches and grapes too, all transported to Les Halles market in Paris.

My dear Richard, if you have held on so far, please continue to read. The most important part is to come. It begins only now and concerns you more than all that came before. That being said I must briefly describe the setting to you, the region and my many agricultural activities, so this story is not suspended haphazardly in a vacuum.

The immense castle of Chinon (12th and 13th centuries) was partially in ruins and overlooked the city. It was located on a hill that rose just in front of the Château de Vaugaudry, which was also situated on a small hill at a distance of about four kilometers. Thus from the heights of Chinon we could see our white castle in the distance and from our house we could contemplate the tall gray ruins of the fortress with its three intact towers where Joan of Arc met Charles VII. Between the two buildings flowed a river, the Vienne, with vast spreading meadows. Willows and poplars lined the river. The single track of a railway bordered the low wall of the property, a secondary line linking Tours to Thouars via Chinon and Loudun; it may still exist. There were usually one or two steam trains a day which were a delight for the children.

Several castles were set on this elongated hill along the Vienne facing Chinon. Vaugaudry, the largest, was surrounded by more land than the others, the whole forming the very beautiful domain of Vaugaudry. We were there in the land of author François Rabelais whose works *Gargantua* and *Pantagruel* contain all the names of places, villages and castles.

Do you know Rabelais? He was — may I say briefly — at the beginning of the 16th century, a sort of Gurdjieff. He designated this region as the center of the world, making Chinon the capital, although he himself practiced medicine in Montpellier and Lyon, lived at the court of François 1er and was parish priest of Meudon. The raspberry-colored Chinon wine renowned since time immemorial provided him with an essential motto: "Always drink, never die." To guzzle and drink for an entire "holy day" was for Rabelais both a feast of earthly pleasures and an abundance of spiritual nourishment. Rabelais' work can be read on several levels. We were thereby installed in the birthplace and symbolic country of François Rabelais, in the "center of the world" in Touraine, the heart and cradle of France.

In 1947, at the end of January my daughter Francine was born at the château and in the spring of 1948 our fourth child was born — my son Sylvain. A midwife from Chinon assisted with both births at home. According to Rabelais we should have baptized them with wine, the famous Breton — BeRRton, as the natives pronounced, the accent very strong on the two RRs. However, to satisfy their grandparents they were baptized with water in Paris. Is that why they cried so much?

Ours was the only large business in this rural area, which kept me busy from morning to night. Touraine, especially around Chinon, was a land of mixed farming, essentially supporting farmers on small, fragmented estates. I was allocated tractors, machines, gasoline and all kinds of material which existed very sparingly in the rest of France.

I was able to obtain this abundance of equipment, although I didn't need it, because of the privileges granted to wounded veterans — thanks to the total absurdity of the French centralized administration, which was very favorable to me. Beginning in 1947 the equipment came almost exclusively from the United States due to the Marshall Plan and was distributed in each department according to the number of its inhabitants. The small farmers around us had no use for large machines or large quantities of equipment, nor the possibility of paying for them even though the prices were advantageous. I had only to choose what I needed, an exceptional situation in those times of shortage.

I could have undertaken a lucrative black market, but I did not think of it, and what some would call my "bad business sense" had the effect of bringing me ten times as much income without machinations or illegal intrigues. I worked very hard and the Lord caused my crops to grow and multiply. The sale of produce was done without difficulty in this post-war period when nothing was available. The merchants took everything we had to sell.

I have described this land of plenty to you, my dear Richard, its main aspects and the many activities linked to it, but I could write a whole book about it. And since this book will never be written, as you well know, let's go together, with Hans-Henning perhaps, to visit Touraine. One day is enough for the round-trip journey from Paris. I'll show you Vaugaudry. There are of course far more heraldic castles placed in more attractive landscapes, but I have never seen a more beautiful property on a more harmonious site.

This letter will go to your address in Munich tomorrow. I thought a lot yesterday and made plans for what I have to tell you. It is not so easy to describe the burst of a totally different level in a daily life that unfolds naturally in a routine ebb and flow. Life does not take place outside of oneself. Life is an inner perception, an inner resonance, whether conscious or unconscious, and it is about this experience that I wish to speak to you, as faithfully as possible without hesitation or reluctance.

You noticed that the stars became more favorable to me, or, if you prefer, that the forces were organized in a more positive way. The dark tunnel of purgatory where I had spent fourteen dark months opened to lighter regions. As I climbed this mount of purification — the ascent of which is not yet complete today, far from it — the horizon widened. Do not let yourself be shocked by these words: stars, planets, purgatory and mount of purification. They concern those who believe in them as well as those who, like you, are skeptical. One merely has to use different words: forces, influences, luck or bad luck, structures, favorable or unfavorable conditions. That said, the mythological form of expression seems to me clearer and easier to access. All this is experienced psychologically, but psychology gives unsatisfactory explanations of the origin of these influences because it elaborates them in its own domain. It is for me like children who want to explain to their parents how babies are made.

The reunion with Ludolf Schild had entered me like a ray of light during the first months in Vaugaudry, while the complete restoration of the fruit estate totally absorbed my strength and thoughts. Ludolf and I only wrote to each other occasionally. The first year, 1946, the harvest was very meager: in other words, non-existent. In the fall, when I was a little freer, a letter from Ludolf arrived. He had been very ill and then had undergone surgery— he did not say for what— and was caught up in great family difficulties. He also wanted to tell me about a certain meeting full of promise and asked me to receive him in Chinon for a stay of about three weeks of convalescence.

I was overwhelmed with happiness and went to pick him up at the railway station in Tours. The road from Tours to Chinon crosses one of the largest forests in France, straight for forty kilometers: the forest of Chinon. Obviously this journey in glorious weather enchanted Ludolf as much as his presence enchanted me. When we arrived on the heights of Chinon, I showed him our white castle in the distance with its domain around it and Ludolf's pale and sickly face already brightened a little.

His presence brought a beautiful harmony to our home; it was a pleasure for everyone. My wife was won over by his natural charm and the delicate way he had of speaking to each of us. He would go to rest for an hour once or twice a day and then accompanied me to my work. We had long conversations. A well-known actor from the *Comédie Française* later told me how much he too enjoyed his conversations with Ludolf Schild.

Ludolf spoke to me at length every evening and sometimes in the afternoon about spiritual subjects, which I saw as before at the Legion, as mere philosophy. I was certainly feeling something else, a deeper impression, yet I was not listening with my full attention. I was not fully available because my mind was occupied with difficulties concerning the workers. Indeed after cleaning, weeding and hoeing all the land, I could not keep all the workers. They all wanted to stay and the choice proved difficult. I finally kept those who knew the work of the vineyard and could quickly learn to tend the fruit trees. Farmers and even winegrowers are generally unaware of fruit growing, let alone intensive growing. However, the solution I adopted made many unhappy.

Ludolf talked with my wife about the same themes but used examples from the education of children. There was a new and unknown intonation in his conversation which gave for me a contemporary taste to our philosophical discussions over the years. He insisted on this relevance and came back to it patiently and appropriately when I continued to remind him of our old exchanges.

Ludolf was certainly the only human being with whom my usual quibbling about always being right gave way and did not lead to endless and useless arguments. He was also the only one I listened to with pleasure, if not with the required attention. Perhaps I lacked the necessary preparation?

He cautiously approached more subtle ideas, telling me of men and women now alive who turned toward wisdom or were deeply connected to it. But I did not ask the necessary questions which would have allowed him to develop the subject further toward finer and more complete explanations. It was probably a disappointment for him. What I was able to grasp later after a certain time had passed shows that no effort in the direction of truth is ever wasted. What is important in this direction is the effort. What matters is the work, not the result, which always remains unpredictable, does not come or comes differently than expected. We can in no way force a future result. On the contrary, too much insistence, too much tension, automatically evokes counterforces and raises adverse opinions. Ludolf, so sensitive and delicate, knew this and in the deep friendship he had for me, he respected this fact. I remember the smiling and friendly way in which he addressed me at the station as he departed: "François I understand, at least partially, that with all this work in the field your mind is not always available for something else. Yet you should learn to keep your attention available and alert to that which is of paramount importance."

From time to time he phoned Paris from the chateau; these calls made him a little sad each time. He explained to me frankly one day that his family took umbrage at the closeness of the relationship that bound him to his students and considered his relationship with the young female dancers too intimate. They visited him every day after his operation and one of them in particular was very attached to him.

He was well-recovered when he left us, looking almost good. Only his eyes retained a certain melancholy. When he beckoned to me from the window of the car as the train moved off, I thought, responding to his smile, how could young women not be in love with this beautiful dancer—so accomplished and so talented? Who wouldn't seek his company?

But he certainly wasn't going back to a bed of roses. His lack of money and the particularly harsh circumstances in Paris made his life difficult. I had to help him.

My in-laws came from Paris every two or three weeks by car, but we had not seen them, owing to various impediments during Ludolf's stay. My father-in-law thoroughly enjoyed the property and his life as lord of the manor more than the harmonious layout of the landscape. He was constantly ready for large expenditures on tractors and other expensive agricultural machinery. The purchase of a good and strong draft horse which he chose himself especially pleased him. He had been raised in the countryside and loved horses. His wife showed her full satisfaction in noting how happily he had been diverted from the stock market business which she considered viscerally detestable. Only our sister-in-law, the wife of Denise's brother, felt unfairly disadvantaged and worried about whether a large caterpillar tractor or any other machine was really needed.

My relationship with my in-laws gradually improved over six months as if swimming in the oil of satisfaction, joy and good mutual understanding. Meeting barely twice a month for two or three days only, rejoicing as the owner of a castle — for yourself and even more in front of others — having fun with your adorable grandchildren, what more could one desire? Their son-in-law was heading in the right direction. He who hadn't decided anything on his own since his return from the war. He had been blamed enough for that and would soon be blamed for the opposite.

On a beautiful, sunny October morning, I was going up to the castle by the main driveway after having assigned the day's work to the different teams, then remaining for a while in the stables which had recently been transformed into a large repair and tool workshop. I was walking between the tall old chestnut trees that had been planted with regularity along the path when suddenly a ray of light reached me. Yes, a beautiful autumn sun was shining. But this light was something else; it had a benevolent clarity. I felt a strange state, unusual, unknown, or almost. I was penetrated by the memory of a cloud of light that had surrounded me once, in February of 1944, at the battlefront in Italy when I was in great danger of death. It was not the same thing, but similar. Walls seemed to widen to let in the light and an interior space grew in this brightness and became more and more luminous.

I stopped spontaneously and stood without moving under a large chestnut tree. Although I was now in the shade, I was just as immersed, just as penetrated by the beneficent light. I remember exactly which tree it was. We had to pass it quickly, especially with the horse because there was a hornet's nest in it. Roger our taciturn handyman who was responsible for the horse, pointed out to me afterward that I should not have remained motionless for so long under this nest of hornets because the stings could be very dangerous. How long did I stay there? I couldn't say, though it was long enough for Roger to mention it to me and it was unusual for him to do so.

I was still under that tree when suddenly the memory of Ludolf came back to me. So, what did he talk to me about? What did he want to tell me?

I realized only then that he had spoken to me of important things which I had not experienced as such at the time and to which I had not paid particular attention. What was it? I almost physically experienced the significance of Ludolf's message but I could not remember its intellectual content. I only knew one thing: this message was essential to me.

I went up to the manor slowly but did not go to my office as usual. I entered the library, the main setting of my conversations with Ludolf, to try to remember, to feel again and above all to reflect. What was the meaning of this experience that I had just had? Was it a question of giving a meaning — no, of finding a meaning, feeling a meaning — of feeling oneself again?

Then suddenly I jumped out of my chair, ran to the telephone and called Ludolf: "It is absolutely necessary for me to speak to you today at your place. I will come in the late afternoon. Please make yourself available. Only you can enlighten me, I have just had a very important experience related to what you said during your visit."

He was surprised on the phone but I said no more. I was in an intensely emotional state but I saw it very clearly. I knew that another decisive turning point was looming but this time it was an inner turning point.

It concerned only me. I informed my wife of my departure to Paris for two days on important business and telephoned my mother-in-law that I would spend the night with them because of issues with our new pump for spraying the trees. It was my first trip to Paris in months and I knew I had to resort to subterfuge. It was later revealed how right I was.

I took my little Peugeot — as old as Methuselah — to Tours, where I caught the train for the Gare d'Austerlitz in Paris.

Chapter V

INNER SPACES OPEN UP

Disabled from war, I traveled pleasantly in first class at a reduced rate. I was reflecting, quietly present to the inflow of feelings, as the train skirted the Loire, this capricious river. Touraine is a land of castles. Not a minute passed without one of them appearing in the landscape, often magnificent and ancient, on the heights or near the track. Between the castle of Amboise, lit by the evening sun above the city where François 1er invited Leonardo da Vinci, and that of Blois, city of "Monsieur," brother of Louis XIV, there was a succession of castles, towers and smaller castles. Then one came to the Beauce, the largest grain region in all of France, where the immense fields had already been harvested. Finally, the houses became more numerous as one crossed into the gray suburbs of Paris.

My thoughts remained with Ludolf. I thought of him and what he had communicated to me a few weeks earlier and which now on the train seemed to offer a great and mysterious promise. I was full of expectation and confidence without impatience, marked by the precious feeling that Ludolf was going to lead me toward something of very high value. I had sensed this from the beginning when we first met in the Foreign Legion. I was certain that he was the only one I ought to listen to, the only one I could trust with an authentic credibility and absolute confidence. He was for me more than a friend — like an older brother of much more mature experience. The masters of India speak of karmic relationships. If such exist, ours was one.

The house where Ludolf lived with his wife Nadia and their

extended family was then more or less settled. It was buzzing like a beehive. Mme. Chipiloff, Nadia's elderly mother, massaged the ladies of Parisian society with full Russian strength. She was known for her vigorous kneading of the fat which she accompanied with *he-hopp-he-hopp* exclamations. As I entered the waiting room I saw a seated row of fat ladies, clearly candidates for kneading, and thin young girls, more likely waiting for their dance or gymnastics lesson. As the only male and the only one standing, I felt a little lost when Mme. Chipiloff opened the door to call her next victim. Our only meeting had been in Algiers two years earlier but she recognized me immediately. Not only in the waiting room but also throughout the house and even in the street her words of welcome in Russian-French resounded in blasts, as if sounded by a trumpet: "Oh! Oh! You brave boy — gave Ludolf rest and recovery — Ludolf very ill, very good dancer but not earning money — Nadia to give gymnastic lessons but must learn first — my grandson Michael, good, cute boy, my darling — you come see Michael."

She abandoned her clients who had obviously heard everything and took my hand to lead me to her grandchildren on the second floor of the house while uttering deafening exclamations on the stairs: "Friend Ludolf, François from grand apple castle has arrived!"

Ludolf and Nadia introduced me to their children: Michael, a truly handsome three-and-a-half-year-old boy, and Luba, an eighteen-month-old baby. Mme. Chipiloff came downstairs trumpeting: "Me, *rabot* (work in Russian) for grandchildren — me better than all young people!"

As the welcome bells of his mother-in-law were ringing, Ludolf was in the midst of giving instructions to his troupe for an upcoming performance while Nadia was taking care of the costumes. I was introduced to charming young people and greeted with smiles and grateful words for having hosted and helped in the recovery of their dance master whom they clearly adored.

"François now belongs to our family," added Ludolf. I also felt that way. I often met with his dance students afterward. Jacqueline, the beautiful dancer with the perfect body, was obviously in love with Ludolf. She was everywhere: She took care of everything in the house, helped the grandmother with the massages, looked after the children and played with them, served as a rehearsal teacher for Ludolf and danced all the duets with him. We quickly became very good friends. Much later this relationship went beyond friendship.

Finding a calm place to talk quietly was not very easy in this effervescence. We were often disturbed. Ludolf looked at me, intensely scrutinizing me with his questioning eyes: "Speak! Tell me, I'm listening to you!" he urged.

I told him what I had experienced that very morning, begging him to explain this mystery and to repeat what he had spoken of in Chinon. What was it really about? Whom had he met? He then replied as follows: "I have tried like you since I was a teenager to develop my potential toward an inner ascent. My beloved mother, may she rest in peace, understood me more-or-less, but my father insisted that I study engineering. It was then that my revolt began because dance attracted me as an expression of the harmony of feelings and their development. I was looking for harmony but found only chaos and cacophony. Even our discussions on philosophy and metaphysics — remember how unsatisfactory they were deep down? We never had any practical indications that would allow us to know how to acquire harmony or wisdom.

"I wandered like you, in the dark, only with more experience and more precise goals. You have often pointed this out to me.

"You wanted to dedicate yourself to medicine and thus to gather knowledge acquired outside of yourself with its applications and make use of it. I wanted to develop my own dispositions and talents within myself. I obviously found masters who taught me to dance, developed my abilities and talent in accordance with the current practice in this art. They were able and intelligent men yet they knew little or nothing about real spirituality. Nadia, despite her constant agitation, is driven by the same quest, although she directs it more toward meeting human beings who are out of the ordinary. This is how already in Algiers and then here we were in contact with a Bulgarian with a large white beard who posed as a master.

"Nadia practices with another pianist who spoke to us one day about a remarkable teaching; at first we did not understand much. She then introduced us to a woman of about fifty of serious and simple appearance. Her name is Mme. Henriette. From the first meeting, her way of being, her attitude and the way she spoke to us made a strong and singular impression. You understand that, don't you? You yourself have just told me that it was the way I spoke to you at the Château de Vaugaudry which that morning gave you such a strong impression of remembering yourself and not what I told you, which you don't remember.

"It has been almost a year since we met Mme. Henriette. I only gradually grasped her presentations and the ideas she developed. It was unlike anything I had ever heard. She constantly returned to the need for a harmonious development of the human being who has in him an aspiration toward high values. It gives the harmony of the human being a very precise meaning because our psychic functions are a trinity: thoughts, feelings and sensations of the body. When any of these three is disjointed and separated from the trinity, disharmony reigns and that is what usually happens. Each of these functions then goes in its own direction independently of the others and often very differently. It is a cacophony which exhausts and nullifies our forces and does not aim at any goal or rather, leads nowhere.

"It is therefore necessary, in order to live and achieve anything, to unite this trinity and actualize the conscious collaboration of these three ordinarily separate functional elements. It is a goal in itself.

"But I am still a beginner, and it is not fair for me to be telling you about fully developed human consciousness awakened to this trinity. I have already said too much — though I see in your eyes, with joy, that all this interests you. You have to see Mme. H. and hear her skillful voice. We are truly grateful and very devoted to her, especially Nadia. She is a simple woman, you know. She leads a modest and upright life.

"I have spoken to her several times about you and our close friendship. I also told her about my cautious but unsuccessful attempt to communicate these things to you. She replied that no sincere attempt is ever unsuccessful but that the result, whatever it is, is not ours. You see, she was right. I see that my speeches had some effect! No man can escape the force of the truth, although the incubation time is different for everyone. There are still many things to say. The best for me would be to introduce you to Mme. H. She already knows more about you than you know yourself!"

I was moved by Ludolf's words and above all by the tact and sensitivity with which he tried to infuse me with something he considered infinitely valuable, and to direct me toward someone for whom he obviously had a very high regard. In short, he was thinking of his friend for his friend's own good. We agreed that he would take me the following Saturday to Mme. H.'s home, quite far in the suburbs, where a few people would be meeting.

It was already late. I rushed to see my parents-in-law, who received me with surprise: One does not deal with agricultural machinery at ten o'clock in the evening. I tried to cling to a grain of truth, explaining that I had met my friend Ludolf Schild, that he had introduced me to his family, that his wife's mother happened to be one of the best and most renowned masseuses in Paris and that the health of Mme. Bretonnière would undoubtedly benefit from massages by this Russian person, a true force of nature. These massages would actually come to pass sometime later for the greater well-being of my mother-in-law, which created for me the most unpleasant difficulties because of complications they brought about.

I excused myself on the following Friday — once again because of the machines that I had to attend to on Saturday. This was again very suspicious, since they knew that businesses were closed on Saturdays. But what aroused their suspicion above all was the new ease and assurance they saw in me.

I went back to Chinon the next day after having actually begun to prepare for discussions about machines at the end of the following week. I also engaged in some new business in Paris, in order to justify my future visits. However, I told my wife sincerely and completely everything that had happened. She was very busy with the children but listened to me with great attention, having high esteem for Ludolf. She agreed to hide our new interest from her parents and to keep it secret.

The following Saturday, Ludolf and I took the train to Épinay-sur-Orge where Mme. H. received us in a somewhat decaying house surrounded by a large green garden. Her gaze was frank and open, with expressive eyes and a face that showed a depth of spirit and also a certain suffering. Separated from her husband, she lived with her seven- or eight-year-old daughter on the first floor of the house in a bedroom and a kitchen which, very simply arranged, also served as a living room. This is where five or six other participants whom she seemed to know well were already seated for the small meeting. She greeted me without the usual polite fuss, examining me briefly in what seemed to me a hopeful manner.

She then sat down on the kitchen table — I remember that precisely — and began to speak. She spoke for a long time. I no longer remember what she said but I do know this: As I listened to her, I felt a beneficent inner expansion, a deep and strong sense of assurance that there was something in me that I could trust completely. I was immersed in this inner benevolence as if in a safe shelter. There I remained silent, absorbed in an interior space that felt intimate yet unknown.

I can still remember: It was the penetration of a new feeling into a formless space, the echo of which vibrated in my heart. It was a "how" and not a "what" that arose as the vibrations resonated from the conversion I was experiencing. As if from afar, I heard Mme. H. inviting us to ask questions. A few people including Ludolf did so. I must have seemed absent because when she turned to me, inquiring if I had something to ask, I jumped but remained silent.

Afterwards she said to Ludolf: "Your friend seems particularly closed."

About a year later she told me that she had at that first meeting felt me to be quite closed, as if sewn up. Later I talked a great deal.

However, I immediately felt that something fundamental had changed, had transformed itself in me. I had found the link that connected me to the event I had experienced at seventeen, so oppressive and so inexplicable. While I had not yet found the meaning of life, I was certain I had found the path that led to it.

On the way back I tried to communicate to Ludolf what I had felt, certainly a very confused attempt. How to speak the unspeakable? Even if he did not understand me, he seemed to perceive my inner change and showed a smiling and silent joy.

Then: "You are introduced," he said to me, "and you can always come back. Hold on to me for a while longer, but soon you'll have to continue on your own. I am very sick. I haven't told you clearly yet but the future of my health is quite uncertain."

It was late 1946 and he had already had his first cancer surgery. I was worried, especially since he was almost exhausted after those two hours with Mme. H. He asked me to accompany him to the University residence hall where he was to give a choreographic show to the students with his troupe. He was leaning on me, merely a half-invalid, and resting on my arm. We arrived very tired and I informed Jacqueline that he could not dance in such a state. But I was wrong. He danced this time and even more intensely during the two subsequent performances. He was dancing — or rather he was flying — filling the space above the stone slabs and stirring up the young spectators with enthusiasm, only to drop after the show, exhausted. When dancing he consumed his deepest forces which were increasingly weak for everyday life, allowing his illness to worsen.

Mme. H. explained it to me during my next visit when I remained alone with her for a whole afternoon: "Your friend is seriously ill. He should take it easy," she told me.

Then she said: "I'm going to give you some private lessons to catch up with the others because the group I would like you to join has been meeting for a year and already knows a certain number of things. Do not change your very valuable countryside activities however. Stay there and continue them."

She insisted and repeated the words "very valuable." Then: "Most of the group members here are occupied with nonsense and engrossed in intellectual hair-splitting. There will now be at least one who struggles with realities, the way a woman who takes care of her grandchildren also faces real things. One can best follow one's authentic aspirations by facing realities."

This language was new to me and at first quite flattering. She also told me that she had been a student of G. I. Gurdjieff, her revered master, since 1939: "G. I. Gurdjieff is of Greek origin, but he was raised in the Caucasus and lived in Moscow before leaving Russia during the revolution. After spending some time in Constantinople and then in Berlin, he settled in France with his students in 1922. Among them was my direct instructor, Mme. de S., who is French. I am sincerely devoted to her; Mr. G. and Mme. de S. have given my life and that of my husband a completely new direction leading to real development."

She sighed: "We were staunch communists and participated in the Spanish Civil War. We led a rather bohemian life. My husband then made the acquaintance of another woman. It's not uncommon and I did not mind. But now I regret it. I know it's too late and I really love him. You at least must be careful not to treat such matters lightly."

She said further: "Your friend Ludolf has a rare and very extraordinary ability to participate in this spiritual search. I have never met a man who has such talent and ability in this sense. What finesse! He is making considerable progress and is already helping me in my own activity.

"Unfortunately, he is seriously ill, more seriously than is generally thought. The first time that Mme. de S., whose judgment is always impartial and in whom I have complete confidence, saw him, she said to me: 'He is a burned man, totally burned.' It's really distressing and regretful because such a talented dancer would be very precious to us in this 'work.' Dances and movement play a big part in it."

Seeing that I had tears in my eyes, she sought to calm me: "We can't say anything; maybe he can still recover. But all the women and girls swirling around him and his perpetually restless wife too are real obstacles to his recovery. The three weeks he spent with you in the country were marvelous for him. You know we are all grateful to you. His wife Nadia is a deeply good person always ready to help everyone, but she is constantly agitated, involuntarily preventing him from resting.

"There is, God be praised, Jacqueline, calm and balanced, very attentive to him, who takes care of everything, not without personal sacrifice. Let's hope that the strength of this frail and sweet girl will hold.

"It is, as you know, a difficult emotional situation for the whole family. I do not have a very easy position there myself, and I am counting on your help. All three—Ludolf, Nadia and Jacqueline—are in my group which meets every Friday evening in a sculptor's studio. You should come there too, according to your possibilities. Try to find a way to come to my house on Friday afternoon. We will talk alone before leaving together for the evening group."

She then explained to me, in clear and concise sentences, the rudiments of the intellectual and theoretical bases of this teaching. She added that this was only a scaffolding for beginners. "The most important thing is always direct experience, which one acquires in life situations. Only what you, yourself, see to be true and correct can convince you and will bring knowledge of real value. Life must, above all, be lived. To approach it theoretically by cogitations of a suspicious subtlety does not make sense. We are however largely absent from ourselves. But to really know, there is only one absolute necessity: to be there, present, to be aware of oneself, to wake up from our hypnotic sleep. You are German-speaking and have a correct word, which we do not have in French: *dasein*. We use only one term, 'work.' As you will see, it is about that, to work, and to also to allow yourself to be plowed. Inner growth requires both outer and inner work. Here again, your mother language helps you. Goethe wrote a sentence rich in practical teaching: '*Was du ererbt von deinen Vätern hast, erwirb es, um es zu besitzen.*' ('What you inherited from your fathers, earn it, deserve it to possess it.')"

Chapter VI
IN THE GROUP OF MME. H.

My dear Richard, you must be aware by now that one of the aims of my life — the most fundamental aim — had changed. My inner atmosphere had shifted as if turning on a hinge, and the dark of my hopelessness disappeared. It opened and lost its gloom. I became freer, surer of myself. After so many meaningless years something had won my confidence, as it did for many others after this terrible war.

I remember a pertinent remark made by one of my group companions: "When you have fallen into the deep crevasse of a glacier, you neither discuss nor judge the color of the rope that has been handed to you; you are only too happy to grab it."

Nonetheless, this was the attitude of certain journalists who endlessly judged and prejudged both Gurdjieff and his teaching.

I had at last met human beings who — with conscience, understanding and sincerity — tried to show their fellow human beings a path out of the chaos toward an order that each could recognize as his own. This filled me with assurance and trust without sentimentality; these were very refined feelings.

At that time however, no books or writings about this "work" existed. Ouspensky's *In Search of the Miraculous* would not be published until the end of 1948, nine months before the death of Mr. Gurdjieff. The transmission was only oral.

Seen from the outside, this was a break in my life. In truth, the awakening that was taking place was gradual and progressive, achieved slowly through experiences that I lived and understood. I was experiencing an initiation in the sense of *initium* in Latin: a beginning. I was starting to walk a solid path firmly convinced that it was leading somewhere. I drew this confidence without a tinge of doubt from the attitude of those who, having been on the path for some time, had already covered a certain distance.

I arranged to come to Paris twice a month and then soon afterward, every week. I left Chinon on Friday around noon and returned on Saturday evening or sometimes later, Sunday or Monday. Destiny came to my help in the guise of a new farm manager from a good agricultural school, who was both passionate and experienced about fruit growing.

Monsieur Lavenne had found the work of his life. He devoted himself to it and although he has now reached an advanced age, he still lives there having well served several of my successors. It was thanks to him that we had our first major harvest of apples in the fall of 1947, around fifty tons, and reached complete financial independence.

I was the one who sold our apples to wholesalers in the Paris market, which completely justified my presence on the market premises at nighttime. Les Halles, belly and bowel of Paris, was at that time a very picturesque institution reminiscent of the Middle Ages. For three years I had adventures there that could fill a book.

My capacity as a fruit grower and farmer which had become somewhat second nature was obviously improving. But Richard, I must tell you an episode from this story. I read many books dealing with intensive fruit growing mostly from the United States. I soon realized that there was no real expert in this field in France and became unsure about how, with only the help of books, I could apply the many measures required by this agricultural endeavor.

The sixty thousand fruit trees at Vaugaudry, more than half of which were still productive, had been planted by the Lepage company, the largest tree nursery in France near Angers. I telephoned Monsieur Lepage, who was of the fourth generation of the family. I met him soon afterward in his office in the middle of the gigantic nurseries and explained my problems to him. He recalled the herculean operation of planting countless apple trees that he had carried out in 1939 and which had put him in the delicate situation of having to plant everywhere, in every possible place as well as impossible. "For considerations having less to do with agriculture than inheritance valuation in my opinion," he said.

All this interested him and he offered to visit me at Vaugaudry, where I was proud to welcome this patrician among nurserymen. Tree nurseries in France draw their prestige from the age of their business because in fact only a good reputation could guarantee the outcomes of tree planting and harvests, as the results are seen only five to seven years later. The Lepage establishment had the best possible reputation. Monsieur Lepage came and visited for a whole day. He examined the entire estate, looked carefully at all the orchards, often taking notes. Later that afternoon we sat in my office and he shared his conclusions with me. Having lived in Anjou for generations he, like me, surprisingly preferred tea to the customary afternoon wine. "I do not need to explain at length," he said. "You are a lucky man. Your immense luck is to have known nothing at the beginning, absolutely nothing, about fruit growing. Everything has succeeded here as much as possible. No professional and experienced man would have ever undertaken the restoration of a fruit-growing estate that had been totally neglected for seven years. None, I am sure. He would have torn out everything, cleaned, prepared the land, planted new trees and naturally would have had no income but only significant expenses. Your ignorance won you the jackpot in this lottery of which you had no idea! And after purchasing the land at the agricultural price and not the price of a fruit growing estate, it is even more than the jackpot. Let us raise our glasses, or rather our cups, to the health of the Vaugaudry estate."

Helpfully, he advised me to uproot a few plots of apple trees and to completely remove the two hectares of peach trees: "Stone fruit trees live much shorter lives and tolerate no neglect. In any case, in a few years (I cannot say how many) these trees which were not properly cared for will no longer bring in anything. Consider replanting early enough to keep a good yield from your superb estate."

Thus I was the big winner of an incredible lottery. I had obtained this reward without suspecting it, completely unaware of any risk. Yet other plans and projects were already germinating within me.

This is how, Richard, after hell and the first phases of purgatory, which is the passage through a dark tunnel of trials, the real ascent of the mount of purification began, an ascent which is not yet completed today.

Beginning in 1947 I followed the instructions of my group leaders seriously and without the slightest reluctance. I do not say "commandments," because they did not order. I had successfully passed one of the tests: I was aware of my total ignorance. Ignorance that has become conscious is significant knowledge.

I followed obediently, carefully, watching the indications in order to discover and understand everything I possibly could. I was participating in an evolution which like all spiritual work was not child's play; it was impossible to take it lightly. As this became clear to me I was completely convinced.

The mount of purification is an absolute necessity. For what? For a surprising reason. Most human beings withstand the worst torments of hell as best they can. Dostoevsky rightly describes man as being capable of getting used to anything, including the worst. On the other hand, strange as it seems, man has difficulty accepting great happiness and felicity. If a living message comes to him from above, from Dante's sky, he is crushed. He takes it as a sign of imminent misfortune, a warning that he will soon have to leave his beloved routine of tranquility.

We often confuse happiness with pleasure and enjoyment. This is an error with catastrophic consequences. This confusion plays a very bad trick on us. Of course, pleasure and enjoyment should be allowed; otherwise frustration builds. And one must understand as quickly as possible not to condemn these desires either in oneself or in others.

I remember the famous Russian physician Doctor Salmanoff,

physician to Lenin and his sister. In 1921 he received a passport from Lenin himself to go to Germany for the sole purpose of perfecting his knowledge of internal medicine in Heidelberg. Later, during the Second World War (from 1939 to 1945) he remained in Paris as a Soviet citizen and had no problem visiting with Germans such as Ernst Jünger. For several years I wrote his endless prescriptions. He was happy to speak in German from time to time in an inimitable way tinged with Russian.

He once said to me, "Grunwald, Grunwald — do a lot of stupid things! Without stupid things, you get nowhere. But act quickly! Do not stop there and don't repeat any of them," he sometimes added. And after a pause to catch his breath: "Sometimes, however, we also have to do something good."

This mount of purification — learning from one's stupidities and mistakes, and from all other experiences — is necessary in order to become capable of enduring happiness. Incredible as it sounds, few human beings can endure true and lasting happiness. An aphorism from Goethe is a reminder of this: *"Alles in der Welt lässt sich ertragen, nur nicht eine Reihe von schönen Tagen."* ("Everything in the world can be endured, except a series of beautiful days.")

Similarly, Gurdjieff stated: "All true happiness experienced is based on unhappiness also experienced."

Later, I was introduced to the wisdom of India, and I would now express this quite differently: Happiness is our true nature, but it is generally unknown by our usual understanding. Here also it turns out that the mount of purification is necessary.

It was in November 1946 I believe, that I came to Mme. H.'s group for the first time, full of expectation. Ludolf, who was ill, accompanied me. Afterward he came only rarely, although some small meetings were held at his home. Nadia and Jacqueline on the other hand, were regularly present, along with fifteen to twenty other people: half men, half women. The group generally met in the workshop of the sculptor Étienne Martin, who was not yet famous. We entered through the courtyard into a picturesque house on an even more picturesque street, rue du Pot de Fer, located in the La Mouffe neighborhood behind the

Panthéon, a bohemian district somewhat ill-famed and rather well-frequented.

We sat on wooden stools and benches between large abstract sculptures in wood and plaster, with white dust everywhere. There was a blissful disorder in the workshop which did not bother the sculptor. On the contrary, Étienne seemed quite proud of it. He greeted me with a frank smile behind an enormous black beard dusted white with plaster. Beard and mustache hid a large part of his face but his eyes shone with a mischievous expression. Étienne Martin, a long-time member of the Academy of Fine Arts, is now globally recognized as one of the great sculptors of our time, and we became true friends.

The people sitting there spoke calmly and quietly, and my arrival caused some curiosity. Then Mme. H. entered and a respectful silence greeted her. She sat in the only wooden armchair, which had been cleaned for her. She sat in silence for some time visibly seeking an inner focus that radiated to all of us. This first time — and again later — I felt the benevolent fullness of this silence in contrast with the silences in society, which were filled with embarrassment or unease.

Mme. H. raised her head to ask a question: "Is anyone willing to recount our current 'work' briefly and to the point for the newcomer, in addition to his own week's work?"

An oral report? There was no response at first, only silence and awkward looks until Jean Planchon raised his hand. He was ready, yes. He was always ready if no one else came forward. Jean was a pharmacist and had been seriously injured during the resistance battles in the Royan region near the Atlantic. There was yet another war invalid in this group named Claude; both men suffered from greater handicaps than mine. I remained good friends with both of them. Claude died not long ago and I saw Jean again recently.

I do not remember what was discussed during this first group meeting. In his book, *In Search of the Miraculous*, P. D. Ouspensky describes the work in the Moscow group between 1915 and 1920 with utmost precision, organizing the subjects by themes yet without specifying how each meeting unfolded.

For myself, I believe that proceeding chronologically would be unsuccessful and probably impossible.

One of the interesting themes of Gurdjieff's teaching deals with "human types." A man's type is innate; he neither acquires nor learns it but comes into the world belonging to a certain type. A few theoretical explanations are sufficient for a schematization of this subject.

There are three types: the intellectual type, the emotional type, and the physical type, which includes moving and instinctive. Trying to classify the people we meet solely according to this schematic system would be a grave mistake, however. First, because we generally meet only mixed types; second and more important, it is one's own type that must be carefully explored; and third, any evaluation requires an extensive experience of several years.

One rarely meets a pure unmixed type. Yet Jean Planchon was an example of a pure "intellectual type"— which is by the way neither an advantage nor a disadvantage, no more than having blond or brown hair, blue or black eyes. Pure types are more common in men than women. Jean spoke in a precise and brief manner without any emotion in his intonations. He was by no means a cold and unfriendly man. On the contrary he was always ready to help and had an easy connection with everyone. But his perception, his understanding, proceeded on an intellectual basis while others arrived at an understanding through feelings or sensations.

This fundamental difference in perception can be a source of great misunderstanding between human beings if they do not gradually learn to take it into account. The "pure intellectual" type does not have anything to do with a particular social or scholarly class, although it is found more frequently among educated people. I also met this type among peasants or workers who rationalized their activities in precisely that way. The "emotional" type appears most often among artists but again, mixed types of all kinds are the most common. "Pure type" simply means a strong preponderance of one of the functions; the other functions are also present in a normal man, naturally. A "pure type" has the advantage of discovering his own type more easily and the disadvantage of having more difficulty in establishing a harmonious balance between his functions.

It would be a great mistake to approach this long task of exploration with a mind filled with preconceived opinions of sympathy or antipathy. Almost everything a man encounters arouses in him attractions and repulsions to varying degrees. These must be observed with objectivity. However, impartially observing one's own bias, while entirely legitimate, is not always easy. We must first recognize the bias. This was a major point that each participant mentioned at that first meeting and in all the following ones. Observe; look impartially; learn to see.

Everyone is biased automatically, and is obliged to be so. It is therefore not a question of rejecting this partiality — denying, judging, or condemning it. It is a question of noticing it. It must enter fully as a fact into our consciousness. We must give it its due before trying to change anything — which in most situations is not necessary if the observation is clear, and impossible if it is not.

Indeed, in the light of consciousness, by virtue of being present to oneself, entirely different processes take place than those that occur in the darkness of non-conscious drowsiness, mistakenly considered our normal waking consciousness. The themes of work, the dialogues and discussions, the exercises, the questions and answers, the weekly "groups" in which I participated for decades, all served this purpose: *Da sein* — to be here, to be present to the processes of one's own life, to grasp their unfolding without the slightest criticism.

But how? How can we escape the twilight drowsiness that we experience as perfectly normal? We called the main task, to be repeated tirelessly, the goal of all the exercises: "to remember oneself!" Self-remembering is this attempt to deliberately remind ourselves of the exile in which we live and to transform it, with the time devoted to this practice, into consciousness.

This idea evoked an immense resonance in me. I had been in exile since I was seventeen, banished. That was the word that explained my very painful state. Of course, I had experienced rejection from my country and emigration as an exile, but this was about my personal homeland, my inner world. I had lost it a long time ago: I lived on the margins of myself. Consciousness was "in exile," captured, stuck in secondary and insignificant circumstances, exiled to the domain of functions and appearances.

Initiating myself into this essential act, carried out intentionally — the "act of remembering" — took some time because I had to familiarize myself with the necessary attitude. I had to remember myself and return for a short moment, from exile to my intimate but unknown homeland — that is to say, to what unbeknownst to me I really am. "I" and "am" were and still are the two key words.

Yet what could be simpler and more obvious than one's own being? There is no possibility of the slightest error because in truth "I am" without any intervention on my part. The rest comes later. Every phenomenon depends first of all on the being of the one who perceives it. But I didn't know that in my life in exile; everything was upside down. With reversal and nonsense come compromises to which one becomes more or less accustomed. I had to transform — to consciously return to myself, make a conversion that was not an allegiance to this or that religious circle, but a return to the truth already existing at the heart of myself.

This approach always faces obstacles. The real enemies are the habits formed over a long time by a perpetually distracting upside-down life that makes us forget the reality of being. Forgetting is the opposite of remembering. Rising up against oblivion to remember oneself was the work, through the call of Mr. G.'s voice and the salutary meditations of Mme. H. that pulled me towards this essence of which I had been unaware.

This was the theme of the "remedial classes" that Mme. H. gave me on Friday afternoons. These sessions were absolutely necessary for me because my group companions were already aware of this main point of the teaching. Certainly one or another of them was only half-aware of his own exile, although this feeling of banishment was the fundamental motive, the condition of his presence in the group and his participation in the work.

It was the first time in a year that someone new had joined the group, which explains the eager and somewhat curious welcome I received. In those days being admitted to a group was quite difficult and many participants had friends or protégés who had been placed on a waiting list. I owed my acceptance to the insistence of Ludolf Schild, who had a privileged position.

This limited enrollment of new people was not based on elite selection however. The simpler reason was the small number of sufficiently trained and experienced men and women capable of transmitting this precious teaching without damage who had been given this task. This remained a difficulty for many years and it is still a problem today. I will come back to this point.

Mme. H. explained this to me and continued by telling me about George Ivanovitch Gurdjieff and how she had met him:

"I was born in 1898 in Orthez, in Béarn, and was raised there in a strict and moralizing Protestant education. My father died prematurely. My mother then earned our living as a peddler to the peasants of the Pyrenees mountains, selling fabrics and sewing accessories, and I accompanied her. These were irreplaceable experiences in this region which until 1914 was completely closed to the modern world. My mother revered the Jews. They were the people of the Bible who served as her model, and Christ was for her the accomplished Jew. I was preparing for the baccalaureate in Bordeaux, and although I was older than my school friends, they mocked me to no end because of my naive and obsolete opinions.

"Later, I became secretary at the International Union of Intellectuals and found myself in contact with budding and established celebrities like Max Planck, Albert Einstein, Marie Curie and Paul Langevin. Then, when I joined the Havas agency as an editor, my horizons were already broadened. It was in this environment of journalists that I became a communist and met my husband Henri, who was ten years younger than I. You will meet him very soon. He is one of the closest French students of Mr. Gurdjieff. We lived through the Spanish Civil War as journalists with the Republicans."

And she told me much about the Spanish Civil War.

"After receiving a small inheritance, we traveled for almost a year throughout South America working for a left-wing Parisian newspaper, and on the way back I became pregnant. Henri had a good school friend, Philippe, son of a psychiatrist and university professor who was overflowing with enthusiasm for all mythologies: Greek, Hindu and others. We had endless discussions with Philippe that could last entire nights.

"'Your communism and all Marxist concepts are pure idiocy based only on wind and errors,' said Philippe.

"And Henri replied: 'These are obviously capitalist opinions. Your mythology only serves to maintain the submission of the masses and to exploit them further.'

"In this way the days passed and the arguments continued to fuel this dialogue of the deaf. But the two men had known and loved each other since childhood. Philippe, annoyed, said one day: 'Do you want proof? I'm going to prove to you that there is a completely different truth, a real one. I'm going to introduce you to someone.'

"'Why not? Your capitalists won't be able to brainwash me.'

"'You will be surprised. These are proofs, I tell you!'

"'Okay, Henri finally concluded, go ahead and set everything up.'

"This is how we met Mr. Gurdjieff and Mme. de S., Philippe's mother-in-law. You will soon know them, too. Mme. de S. and Mr. Gurdjieff are my revered masters. I won't tell you anything about them; it's useless, you'll see them. Mr. G. is a surprise for everyone. In his impossible Russian-French, he had no difficulty in confusing and bamboozling my Henri, who was so educated by books.

"Since the beginning of 1939, we have both been his students, diligent in this intense work on ourselves. For two years Mr. G. has charged us with founding groups to bring him qualified and prepared students. We had never considered it and were hesitant at first, but it was a required task. Because I am trying to assume this responsibility myself, I am only beginning to understand his teaching more accurately. I am deeply grateful to him."

This is how a relationship of intimate trust was established between Mme. H. and me. I felt great respect for her and was grateful that she spoke so openly about her own life. She told me many details of her life which do not need to be mentioned here. The naturalness and frankness with which she communicated her deepest experiences and the events she was going through gave rise to a particularly warm human relationship between her and the members of the group. She participated in our lives and we participated in hers.

At the beginning of 1947, Mme. H. told me that few people in the group had met Mr. G. and that among them Ludolf alone had grasped the greatness and value of this man. Others had been strangely surprised and intimidated and somehow disconcerted. But Ludolf, because of his illness did not want to go to Mr. G.'s often, and it was a shame because he could have, as he lived very close. Mme. H. quoted Ludolf as saying: "Mr. G.'s home is not a place for sick people. Before, it was different, but now it seems to me that I would only be an obstacle for him."

And no argument from Mme. H. could make him give in once he had decided. "But it will soon be your turn," added Ludolf.

First, I had to be introduced to Mme. de S.

One day Lise, Mme. H.'s niece, came to visit her aunt. She helped Mr. G. at home. He himself prepared meals or feasts every day at lunch and dinner for around fifty people, sometimes more.

"He is an extraordinary cook who knows how to treat his guests to delicious oriental dishes," Mme. H. told me. "Throughout the war, his house was the only place where I could eat properly, and it still is. I think without him I would have died of starvation.

"I heard that you grow apples," Lise told me. "Could you bring one or two crates to Mr. G.? I don't think he eats them himself, but we all love them, and we can hardly buy good apples."

I was happy with the request and delighted to fulfill it.

Chapter VII

MEETING WITH GURDJIEFF

The meagerness of the first harvest in the fall of 1946 left me with only a small reserve of apples and little money by the beginning of 1947. I did not want to go into excessive debt, yet I absolutely wanted to help Ludolf and Mme. H. financially. Both of them were living in conditions bordering on poverty while I was swimming in abundance.

Thus I decided, without the slightest scruple, to take advantage of the black market. I asked the Agricultural Service of the prefecture of Tours to grant me a large number of gasoline vouchers for my machines and motor vehicles. Most of them in fact consumed diesel which I had in sufficient quantity. Gasoline was rare at that time and sparingly distributed through a system of vouchers allocated by the different administrations. I expected that about a quarter of my request would be satisfied, but when I was on my way to Paris with two crates of my finest apples, I stopped in Tours and was given all I had asked for. In Paris our clever cinema director, Mr. Villiers, transformed my fuel tickets into a very nice sum, not without giving himself a percentage in the process.

"Live and let live," as my father used to say.

I offered half of this money to Ludolf and the other half to Mme. H. Surprised and embarrassed by the size of these donations at first, they laughed indulgently afterward when I explained the origin of the money.

Lise had informed me that Mr. G. generally went out between ten o'clock in the morning and twelve noon. So I arrived around eleven o'clock at his apartment on rue des Colonels Renard without any apprehension or hope of meeting him. When I rang the doorbell, I heard the sound of shuffling footsteps behind the door and surprise! He himself opened it. It could only be he: this large forehead and skull as shiny as a billiard ball without the slightest trace of hair. When one met Mr. G. for the first time it was this skull that one noticed first, the most striking external aspect, always and for everyone.

He was wearing an indoor jacket and slippers. His large black eyes, with their extraordinary expression, seemed to be questioning me. My dear Richard, I will try to describe these eyes to you! They revealed a serenity from which radiated intense affliction, a sort of sacred sorrow, along with an ironic malice. One could see many other things there, but this deep pain perceived by so many others was always present.

Mr. G. looked at me questioningly. I was showing him the two crates of apples when Lise arrived and explained. Then with a broad gesture he invited me in, carefully examined the apples, and signaled for me to follow him into a small windowless storage room where shelves surrounded a narrow sofa, like a sort of library. Instead of books however, the shelves held precious foodstuffs selected with care and taste. Choice edibles, colorful chocolate bars, liqueurs, very beautiful bottles of brandy, rare preserves, dates and dried figs, candied fruits — large and small, red, green and purple and much more. Other prettily packaged foodstuffs sat side by side as if in a presentation of sweets arranged by a decorator.

Mr. G. sat down on the sofa, legs crossed Turkish style and motioned for me to sit on a stool. A small and graceful table inlaid with ivory separated us. Then he spoke to me in Russian-French far from anything grammatical: "Mme. S. not talk about you. You know Mme. S.?"

"No," I replied. "I met Lise last week at Mme. H.'s house. I am a student of Madame H."

And he: "Ah! Henriette, that very good person, you are lucky. Do you have a wife and children? Do you live in Paris?"

"No, I am a fruit grower in the countryside. I am married and I have three children. The last one was born recently."

He gazed at me with a particularly kind smile: "Ah! Thus a father of a family, a responsible person, not a young scoundrel. First talk to Mme. S. then come to my house. Only Mme. S. let parasites come in. Guests, I invite myself. You student of Henriette, already candidate for parasite."

He took a large bar of chocolate and three small ones from a shelf and handed them to me: "Large chocolate for mother from me; a small chocolate for every child from me; the smallest must also eat; very good chocolate. You will come back, but first speak to Mme. S."

He stood up. Only then did I notice his large white mustache, the tips of which curved carefully upwards. I also saw that he was relatively small, strong and stocky; his eyes alone had attracted me at first. He accompanied me to the entrance where Lise whispered in my ear, smiling: "How relieved I am! I was really afraid he would throw you out. How many times has he already done it for unwelcome people. It's a coincidence that he's here this morning."

I had not expected this encounter at all but it had aroused in me neither embarrassment nor shyness. On the contrary, I felt very free and filled with a great and natural respect. A man full of wisdom, a sort of oriental sheik, had welcomed me and visibly expressed his benevolence. That evening at the group dinner he apparently said to Mme. H: "Today your apple student came here."

I came regularly to Paris during the winter and spring to participate in the Friday evening group at Étienne Martin's on rue du Pot de Fer. Little by little I began to ask questions and receive answers and suggestions for the exercises that were offered to us each week. I applied myself to carrying them out in order to train my still lazy power of attention.

I soon observed that each discovery made me progress one step forward, provided that it was spontaneous. What I forced in contrast became artificial and misleading. Any tension, any impatient expectation, inevitably led to an impasse. One of my first discoveries surprised me a lot. It often happened that after having prepared myself precisely for a question or an observation in the group, having even chosen the words to formulate it, a completely different remark came out of my lips, spontaneously expressing more accurately my real problem and to which I received a satisfactory answer. And what I had prepared in such detail suddenly seemed stale.

The exercises we were given only have meaning in a particular context, so describing them here would not make sense. Unfortunately, this caused misunderstandings which, sometimes, some people kept alive — those who for example listened without intelligence to the directions that were given and became their victims. In this regard I am thinking of one or another person in Germany,[1] especially one.

From Monday to Thursday, I worked eagerly and efficiently at the Vaugaudry estate. On Friday morning I took the train from Tours to Paris and returned to Chinon late on Saturday evening. My wife also became interested in the "work" because of me at first, then for herself, and especially after Mme. H.'s two-week stay at the castle.

It was during the summer of 1947 when extraordinary heat filled the air. We had cut the green branches too early and the sun burned the apples with black spots. We feared losing them all. However, it was temporary, and only the summer fruits suffered. The others ripened properly and gave a large harvest in the fall.

Mme. H.'s stay, although strewn with unpleasant incidents, or perhaps because of them, taught me and helped me a lot. My wife Denise was extremely happy that the "work", about which she had heard so much — from me and especially from Ludolf — came in person to her, home delivered, so to speak. Mme. H.'s visit also had this aim and Denise knew to appreciate it. From the first day our teacher took care of her during the day, and of me in the early evening after my activities around the estate.

---

[1] François Grunwald led Gurdjieff groups in Germany during the 1970s.

Out of compassion Mme. H. had brought one of her students with her, a young woman whose husband had just left her and who Mme. H. believed should not be left alone. She apologized at the station and said to me in front of the young woman: "Let me introduce you to Suzie, intermittently depressed. Like chronic drinkers, she slips every three months into a crisis. I couldn't leave her alone."

Mme. H. was like a helpful and tireless Saint Bernard, sensitive to people's misfortune and always ready to help extract them from trouble. She had therefore taken Suzie into her home — just as she had during the war hosted and hidden with incredible difficulty the four members of a family of Polish Jews. Then after the war, she had taken in a few more people, who this time were wanted for their collaboration with the Germans. I was sure that she had passed the money I gave her on to some needy people.

The first two days of her visit passed without incident, beneficial and pleasant. Then the morose face of our neurotic Suzie darkened hour by hour until it became really dark. She was frustrated, craving constant attention from Mme. H. and gripped with all sorts of jealousies, the poor thing. She let it all out on the third day in the form of a crude accusation against her own parents, whom she cursed and called by the filthiest names. According to her they were the dregs of the human race. My wife, upset that anyone would speak like this about their own mother and father, became angry. She violently defended the absolutely respectable character of parents. A wild argument arose between the two women. I tried to intervene but in vain. They did not want to hear me. Mme. H. listened, visibly interested. I could see that without taking part in the quarrel she was on Denise's side. After a while, when the excitement had turned into fury, Mme. H. took the crying Suzie by the hand, led her outside, plunged her head into cold water and lectured her sternly. Denise was sobbing and calmed down with difficulty.

This episode gives me the opportunity to indicate Mr. G.'s views on this subject. As I heard myself and as others reported to me, Mr. G. frankly conceded that he totally lacked understanding of the attitude of many people from the West, including some of his students, toward their parents: "I grew up in Armenia and the Caucasus, he said in substance. There parents are sacred, and we do not allow the slightest disrespect toward them. We would feel guilty for not loving them sincerely. What I see here makes me want to stop talking about it. However, I must tell you a very important point: never, ever, should you do an exercise given by me or suggested in a group with your own father or mother. You can use all other human beings but never your father or your mother, whether they are alive or already dead. There are no exceptions to this rule."

He sometimes added: "Yes, yes, I know that many come to me because they are looking for a father. At first that doesn't matter. But you definitely have to learn to make real relationships with your parents whether still living or already gone. Otherwise, no salvation!"

And then, using a solemn tone, in his inimitable Franco-Russian style he said one day: "Mother and Father make a big hole in the sky." He raised his arm with the index finger pointing upwards. "Through this hole you pass to go to heaven; no other way to heaven than the hole made by parents." Then slowly chanting in his deep voice, "Amen!"

Mme. H. soothed my wife with this point of view. Suzie calmed down after this incident and curbed her latent excitement. Still, as a common German proverb says:

Man soll den Teufel nicht an die Wand malen.

Literally: "One should not paint the devil on the wall." And in French: "One does not talk about rope in the house of a hanged man".

Two days later my in-laws showed up without warning, as usual. They knew nothing of the presence of our guests, yet the perceptive Mme. Bretonnière had been smelling something for some time; certain signs seemed very suspicious to her. Weren't we — Denise, the children and I — HER property? I can say in all honesty that my inner, mischievous Viennese nature made itself known in an associative way, by steering the drama towards humor and whispering in my ear: "Father and mother, I can believe it! But mother-in-law?!"

There were mutual introductions along with dark looks from the "owner of our lives and destinies." There were neutral or falsely sweet exchanges. My mother-in-law followed the bonton habits of good society by repressing or withholding any snarl or question. At dinner the frozen silence of my father-in-law, to which we were more or less accustomed, grew a few degrees colder. Fragile Suzie probably searched the dining room floor for cracks in which to hide.

M. Bretonnière quickly got out of this embarrassment by playing and spending more time than usual with his grandchildren. Jean-Pierre was five years old. He loved his grandpa, a man with a great kindness of heart deep down, who used his silence to mask the fact that he was embarrassed to speak. Marie-Claude, at two years old with her very curly black hair perpetually in disarray, was the cutest and most mischievous little girl there ever was.

Mme. H. had inherited from her native region a character trait common to the people of Béarn: courage mixed with diplomatic finesse. With relative success she surrounded the dowager mother with discussions about Béarnaise cuisine and bamboozled the grandfather by talking to him about his grandchildren. Being able to enter into a conversation with her enchanted my father-in-law, a man whose inner stiffness often excluded him from this kind of activity. Thus passed without much pain three days with my in-laws. Mme. H. often accompanied me to the orchards and fields and took more interest in farming activities.

All this however, greatly displeased my mother-in-law, and we could henceforth count on difficulties from her. Believing that we were adhering to a new religion, she was very upset and reproached us for it. She had never cared about her own Catholic religion, but it was part of the usual and generally appreciated social mores and had the advantage of making the pastry shops flourish, at least on Sundays and holidays.

Mme. H.'s stay continued without difficulty and was fruitful for us. We agreed upon her departure that our entire group would stay at the castle for five or six days the following spring. We could accommodate twenty people and this retreat took place the next year. Suzie thanked us exuberantly, apologizing for her outbursts of negative emotion.

Chapter VIII
THE CIRCLE OF IDIOTS

Mme. de S. had the attitude and bearing of a queen. Her simple behavior and direct way of expressing herself without artifice or emphasis further added to this noble distinction. One was immediately attracted by her graceful manner of moving, as well as her straightforward way of speaking. Her beautiful face and her dark, kind eyes commanded respect.

When I first met her she was fifty-seven years old. Even now, almost a century old, she retains this regal appearance. This is almost a miracle and makes her, with utmost respect, an exemplar of the kind of school to which she devoted her life. I saw her again in May 1987 during the public screening of a film about the Gurdjieff Movements[1] and can attest to this once more.

In those early days, Mme. de S. lived in a relatively small apartment that she sublet from one of her students, where she received me for the first time. This residence as well as its decoration appeared to me simple and elegant, in perfect taste. She said: "Henriette has already told me a lot about you but perhaps you could tell me more?"

I do not know why, but I spontaneously told her of my buried desire to study medicine, confessing the importance it held deep in my heart.

She was surprised: "However, you are successfully growing apples on a large scale and you already have three children and perhaps a fourth will come."

Today I find this remark startling because in fact Sylvain, the

[1] The sacred traditional dances brought by Gurdjieff, referred to as "the Movements."

youngest of my children, was born a year later. Then she said: "I will introduce you to Michel, my son. He is currently finishing his medical studies."

She went to get him. Michel was a handsome young man, very distinguished, to whom a mustache and a slightly swarthy complexion gave a somewhat Asian appearance. Conversation moved easily between the three of us about medical studies and other matters.

Mme. de S. then explained that she had assembled all of Mr. G.'s French students and gradually brought them together. He had returned to settle in Paris at the beginning of 1939 after a long stay in the United States. Only the French were able to meet with him during the war. Later, when the hostilities ended, his American and English students began arriving in large numbers. The French were willing to make room for those who had been deprived of his presence for so long and came less frequently to his home for lunch and dinner.

Mme. de S. added: "There are already many of us, and we are cramped because the apartment is small. Come tomorrow evening. I carefully choose the participants at the meals in order to create the necessary atmosphere for the work being undertaken at that moment. If you want to share Mr. Gurdjieff's table when you come to Paris at lunchtime or in the evening, call me. I will arrange it according to what is possible."

There was no elevator. I walked down the six flights of stairs, dazzled to have been received in such a natural and unpretentious manner by a lady of such distinction.

The following visits taught me a great deal. Along with five or six other newcomers from the provinces, I benefited from more opportunities than the Parisians. The material well-being of provincials in the post-war period exceeded that of the city dwellers in Paris who were forced into heavily reduced circumstances and a difficult material life. Perhaps like the Americans, we provincials had more resources. For example, the administration awarded me quite officially, and without any trickery, a large Peugeot at the normal price, something unthinkable in Paris and therefore a rare item. I sometimes used this car to take Mr. G. or Mme. de S. shopping.

I spent a lot of time in Mr. G.'s small apartment on rue des Colonels Renard during the last years of his life and for fourteen years after his death. The arrangement of objects and furniture was always the same. From the very first evening I received an impression there that remained strong and never faded during my subsequent visits.

Many people crowded into the room, some seated close together on a carpet on the floor, others on a large green velvet couch. There were also a few chairs for the disabled. Next to the entrance there was a small armchair also green, visibly waiting for Mr. G.; Mme. de S. was seated in a corner. We listened to the reading of a manuscript. Although about to burst, the place continued to fill. People kept arriving and inexplicably managed to find places. Finally, the door was opened wide and the entrance hall filled as well. I knew almost no one, with the exception of Mme. H.

All kinds of framed paintings and drawings lined the walls of this little living room without leaving a gap. On one side a mirror lay flat on the floor with a display case framed by glass shelves placed on top of it. Small, finely crafted figurines covered everything: the mirror, display case, and shelves. There were tiny, harnessed carriages, all types of peasants and soldiers, and countless miniature dolls dressed in a variety of colors in different outfits and postures. I was sitting on the carpet close to this display and was careful not to jostle anything. This absorbed me so much that I was distracted from listening to the difficult text that was being read and about which this first time I understood almost nothing.

Then Mr. G. entered. With a nimble movement he seated himself upright in the chair and looked attentively at each person. As he said later, he was observing the expressions of the listeners to see the effect of his writing on their faces.

After an hour and a half the reading stopped. It was ten o'clock. Whispers began. Mme. H. approached me and told me of her satisfaction at seeing Mr. G. finally recovered from a recent car accident which had seriously disabled him. His movements and his attitude showed the improvement in his condition. She added: "Be careful. Although this first time you are permitted to orient yourself, next time you will have to choose an 'idiot.' Mr. G. will certainly tell you that himself but with a person like you from the countryside, I am cautious and letting you know ahead of time."

I obviously did not understand her and went from one surprise to another all evening. The person and the radiance of Mr. G. made a striking impression on me. My inner experience was filled with a kind of formless, unfathomable, benevolent depth that is very difficult for me to describe, the taste of which remained afterward and even intensified.

Mr. G. was sitting, legs crossed in the Turkish style, on a small green sofa near a corner of the table. Several minutes of silence passed during which the small dining room became filled with a sacred respect — a respect that seemed to be directed toward the atmosphere itself, rather than toward the man. Then full plates of soup were passed silently from hand to hand, from the kitchen to the table and then to each individual. This was followed, still in total silence, by other plates containing rice, vegetables, meat minced into balls and finally Middle Eastern desserts.

Mr. G. then spoke to a man sitting close to him who was busy filling glasses with various kinds of alcohol, asking each person which one he or she wanted: red or white vodka, armagnac, cognac, calvados and others. "Mr. Table Director, get to work!"

Then he turned to me. I was standing across from him against the fireplace mantle on which I had set my plate: "You, new. Not guest, but parasite candidate. Guests come only once or twice, to eat and drink. Parasites - those who want to work, want to learn this. If you want to become a parasite and not just a candidate or a guest, then next time, choose idiot. But choose for yourself. Obligation for you. Don't tell anyone about this."

And he repeated louder: "Tell no one." Then, "Forward, Director!"

THE CIRCLE OF IDIOTS

This man, the Table Director, offered successive toasts spaced a few moments apart as we ate in silence:

> 1. To the health of all ordinary idiots! he said loudly, raising his full glass to each of the participants who had chosen to place themselves under this name.
> 2. To the health of all superior idiots!

And the ceremony went on:

> 3. To the health of all arch-idiots!
> 4. To the health of all round idiots!
> 5. To the health of all square idiots!
> 6. To the health of all recalcitrant idiots!

To which Mr. G. added in a strong voice: "To the health of all hysterical women!"

> 7. To the health of all hopeless idiots!

Then, Mr. G. quite solemnly chanted the following words: "If there is no hope, then only continue to work always, working internally without hope of result. Work, work always brings results, often later, great result, then great profit, much greater than all expectations."

He sometimes added incitements that I will probably mention when the time comes.

> 8. To the health of all compassionate idiots!
> 9. To the health of all enlightened idiots!

There were other idiots rarely chosen at that time, and for this reason I have unfortunately forgotten them.

Mr. G. turned to me again: "Did you listen? Out of all the idiots next time you choose. Myself: idiot number 18. God also: idiot number 21."

My friend Richard! You can imagine how disconcerted I was, although pleasantly disconcerted, so to speak. I was aware of having been drawn into an adventure, and this adventure awakened my desire and thirst for knowledge — as if a great naiveté, or perhaps an innocence, or a mixture of the two inhabited me — and I am grateful for it. It made me open to experiencing these situations — to my advantage — and kept me from subjecting them to criticism.

Besides, on what criteria could I have based the slightest assessment? After the persecution and violent events of the war, such ceremonies could not intimidate me in any way. They rather intrigued me and I found myself drawn into the game. Any criticism became not only superfluous but absurd. My presence at this surprising ritual came from my will: I was there because I wanted to be there! Yet a number of my group companions spoke of these evenings with a restraint that bordered on fear or even repulsion, which surprised me. It all seemed very foreign to them, and this was one of the reasons that so few new students presented themselves to Mr. G.

In addition, space was lacking. A maximum of eighty people could enter this apartment, and only on the condition of remaining motionless. No question of moving! Thus a selection was naturally established. Nevertheless, those who did not want to come remained devoted to Mme. de S. and the elders who instructed them.

Subsequently, I participated quite often in dinners and sometimes came to midday meals after asking permission from Mme. de S. each time. Later, after certain things happened Mr. G. himself gave me authorization to come at any time, like his long-time students.

For my second visit, I arrived earlier so I could sit on the carpet in a place that allowed me to hear and see better. M. Henri continued reading the manuscript. This French translation would later be used for the publication of the main book written by Mr. G., *Beelzebub's Tales to his Grandson.*

Henri read remarkably well, in a distinct, clear and restrained voice tinged with emotional vibrations. Mr. G. listened for some time before interrupting: "I don't understand French well, but he a very good reader; he always reading, good vibrations, I can see on faces."

I listened, and my attention gradually sharpened as I became more and more captivated by the reading. It was an impressive text, Chapter XXV of the first book, "The Most Holy Messenger from above - Ashiata Shiemash." Once again Mr. G.'s eyes went from one face to another. It was not bothersome, quite the contrary. This look seemed to strengthen my attention to the reading. From then on I became an enthusiastic listener and reader of *Beelzebub's Tales*.

However, this text repelled many of my group companions. Even Mme. de S., who had directed the superb French translation with Henri, was not, it seemed to me, passionate about the book. I became convinced of this during the discussions we had on the subject of producing a German translation. Philippe, her son-in-law, admitted to me one day that reading *Beelzebub* made him physically uncomfortable and even sick to the point of vomiting. Yet human beings are so diverse that the book also had a large number of enthusiastic fans, especially among the Americans. In any case, reading this book is revealing in the sense that it acts directly on the listener or reader, sometimes generating a physical sensation.

Richard! I have just placed a copy of *Beelzebub* in front of me to check the spelling of certain names, and once again the photograph of Mr. G.'s head, taken by my late friend Andrieux, strikes me. This is exactly how he looked: his eyes, his moustache, and his shiny skull which reflected the light. You too must put this photo from the book in front of you when you read about the daily feast at his table. Do it for him who no longer frequents the soil of this earth.

Journalists have the peculiarity — shared by many others, to be fair — of having a particular veneration for the dead. Only then do they recognize their greatness. However, it was given to me to love and follow great living men — and not only Mr. G., who caused the shift, the turning point, in my inner life. Seek also to meet and venerate living men; it is a more fruitful direction for one's growth.

The table in his apartment was set. At least thirty small glass containers with Russian hors d'oeuvres (*zakouskis*), cups of crème fraîche and various sauces were spread out in front of him as he sat on the cushioned sofa. Older people and invited guests occupied most of the chairs around the table. Mme. de S. faced him. Next to her was Mme. H. I stood next to Mme. H., squeezed with the others around the large rectangular table, in the middle of a crowd that stretched from the living room to the entrance.

Mr. G. sat very straight. An irresistible calm emanated from him. Gradually a silence arose, becoming more and more dense. A majestic grandeur without material or psychological limits circulated and settled in our exterior and interior spaces. Our attention sharpened as all sensation of time receded. Everyone, more and more established in themselves, looked at Mr. G.

I am now convinced that what was clearly experienced as an inner majesty did not emanate from him as a person. Rather he was a kind of channel, a path to access something higher that he made perceptible. His presence was the necessary transformer, allowing a submersion into this vastness, this immensity, where my own thoughts no longer bothered me as they usually did but simply withdrew. Mr. G. provided a passage to inner greatness, and that is why I revere him. However, I did not recognize it at the time. This image of a transformer did not come to me until much later. It was a point of view that proved extraordinarily fertile for me.

Of course, I cannot describe, explain, or comment on what it gave access to. Even so, I can tell you how he brought us closer to this unspeakable and inexpressible truth through a seemingly banal story:

> During the great massacre of 1943, with war everywhere, I tried to eat in the large brasserie, Place Clichy. I look at the menu and see: "onion soup." Very happy, love onion soup. Order from waiter and look forward to it. Large steaming plate, I taste it, no taste of onion! Call waiter

and say: no onion taste, no onion in there! And boy answers: It's war, sir, no onion, it's onion soup without onions. I am amazed; think a lot. Always everywhere, onion soup without onion! You come here, rue des Colonels Renard, the only place where onion soup with onion.

No comment, my dear Richard, and too bad for those who don't understand. I searched a lot and for a long time afterward to find onion soup with onion. How rare is this taste! I only understood gradually that all my dissatisfaction, singular and plural, was due to this lack and the ineradicable nostalgia for the authentic onion. But in the war of all against all, real onions are becoming rare and ersatz ones are flourishing.

Let us return to the meal with Mr. G., whose whole person remained imbued with this strong presence.

With calm gestures he placed small bowls in front of him and prepared cold salads, each one different. He mixed olives, pickles and radishes, spices and herbs, chives and parsley, small pieces of smoked fish or meat and other ingredients in a bowl, then poured cream or sauce into it and offered it to one or another of us. He gave one to Mme. H., who passed it to me, and his gaze focused for a moment on her and me.

Please do not think that I was in a trance-like state. On the contrary, my mind was clearer than ever. No exhilarating emotion invaded me, a feeling of true security prevailed, a taste of lived reality. It was from these moments that the difficult discrimination between emotions and authentic feelings began in me, a subtle discernment which is the first step toward knowledge of the delicate emotional field.

Full plates were then passed from one person to the next: first the soup, then the main course of vegetables accompanied by various meats and finally the desserts. I was extremely hungry and did not deprive myself of eating with appetite.

After the soup, Mr. G called: "Come on, table director."

"To the health of all ordinary idiots!"

There were many candidates. Director Bernard Lemaître,

may he rest in peace, filled several glasses. We had to drink a whole glass for each toast. When I asked for red vodka, Mr. G. stopped the table director's hand. "That, filth for Parisian snob. You take armagnac, that good juice. To the health of all superior idiots!"

I had, I don't know for what actual reason, chosen this idiot; perhaps because it was Mme. H.'s. I don't have the slightest idea. Mr. Gurdjieff then commented: "That, good idiot for you."

And to my great astonishment, he said to me, in German with a Russian accent: *"Wissen warum guter idiot? Lokomotifconduktor and Oberlokomotifconduktor!"* (In German, every superior is always *"ober"*. In French, one says "chef.")

He continued, "Do you know why he's a good idiot? Locomotive driver and Chief locomotive driver!"

I understood that this "idiot" referred to those who carried within them the secret or deliberate desire to always be above others.

Then came the circle of idiots: the arch-idiot, the round idiot, the square idiot. After the toast to the recalcitrant idiots, Mr. G. generally added: "To the health of all hysterical women!" And, "That bizarre idiot, always changing like good and bad weather. Once wanting to work, once not wanting."

At the mention of hopeless idiots, he would stand up and with burning eyes utter the phrase I have mentioned above. Sometimes it changed a little. This time he added solemnly: "Who always works hard on himself, without compromise, can die in peace like a true man. Who doesn't work dies like a mangy dog."

He repeated with a frightening grimace: "Die in the dirt like a mangy dog."

A woman raised her glass: "To the health of all the enlightened idiots! To the health of all compassionate idiots!"

Mr. G. added, looking at her intensely: "And to your health Mme. de S., and he whispered something to her in Russian."

That evening and on other evenings, I drank seven or eight glasses — not liqueur glasses, but small glasses, of Armagnac, without feeling the slightest intoxication or feeling sick to my stomach, or anything unpleasant, nor even an exuberant or suspicious euphoria.

Mr. G. poured into his own glass the contents of a dark bottle that he kept next to him. Was it alcohol? I don't know, although I tend to believe it was. He encouraged everyone to drink, sometimes quite insistently, always with this recommendation however: "Only here at my house you have permission to drink like this. Not outside."

Some of the older students like Mme. de S. or Mme. H. only touched their glasses with the tip of their lips, but he seemed to choose not to notice it. Midnight had already passed. One or another person would get up and leave discreetly. Mme. de S. left and many others followed her. A few still remained when I too left.

Outside it was a foggy night. I walked for an hour or two, wandering the streets around l'Étoile and l'Avenue de la Grande Armée before returning to the small room that Ludolf and Nadia had lent me in their house. The next day I told Ludolf as much as possible about what I had experienced the previous evening. He listened to me with satisfaction, assuring me that he too had experienced similar events at Mr. G.'s and he was only waiting for his health to improve before returning there. Unfortunately, he was not well at all.

I have pondered, thought and rethought for years about this remarkable ceremony, trying to find plausible and adequate explanations. I hesitate, Richard, to communicate my conclusions to you for fear that they will create more misunderstanding than clarification. Mr. G. once indicated that a ritual that was transmitted without error through the centuries could replace entire libraries. Likewise, Mme. de S. declared: "The entire life and each of the gestures of a fully developed man made whole by such a development are rituals."

These two statements seem true to me. Whether the account of a ritual is justified and useful is already a question. Whether the commentary and explanation of such an account are also useful is another question far more problematic and uncertain.

Chapter IX
A DOUBLE LIFE

Dark storm clouds were gathering which soon streaked across the family sky with angry lightning, heralding the heartbreaking crashes that were to come.

My mother-in-law learned that I often came to Paris without visiting her. This happened innocently, without a detective or any kind of investigation, while she let herself be kneaded and rubbed down by Nadia's mother, the masseuse. What did they discuss during these intimate moments? The two mothers-in-law did not have many mutual subjects. The one who liked me told the other, who barely tolerated me, everything she knew about me.

A little later I brought my wife to Paris without going to see her parents. Their cries and reproaches, more deafening than thunder, affected Denise quite painfully but left me indifferent. In any case, the apple harvest was abundant in the fall of 1947, which finally gave me financial independence and required my presence in Paris.

Another time my wife attended a dinner at Mr. G.'s apartment. Mme. de S. welcomed her with respect and Mr. G. treated her, it seemed to me, as a guest. She was deeply touched certainly, although her experience, which I have no right to speak of here, took a direction significantly different from mine. The family storm again brought forth its thunderbolts, but the fire was short-lived; when there was no more straw left the fire went out. Denise sincerely loved her parents and expressed this to them. Furthermore, my intelligent mother-in-law instinctively knew that her excessive rage fueled by her acute sensitivity could jeopardize her relationship with her grandchildren, whom she adored. She calmed down, deducing from her Parisian experience that some sort of affair, as was common among those around her, was occupying me in the capital.

As a result, my in-laws no longer rewarded me with advantageous credits or funds. This new status quo considerably facilitated my decision to leave the Château de Vaugaudry three years later, a decision that almost everyone, including my own children, disapproved of and for which they subsequently reproached me.

Two desires motivated my resolution, however. First, I wanted to live in Paris permanently in order to participate more intensely in the groups and finally resume my medical studies. And second, the financial potential of Vaugaudry was not sufficient to justify the investments needed to sustain it. The vigor and yield of the apple orchards were coming to an end. The necessary uprooting of old apple trees and large-scale planting of new trees would mean years without revenue. Where would I have found so much capital? My successors at Vaugaudry carried out this work, effectively leaving them for several years without a harvest.

Mephisto with *Faust* refers to himself as: "*Ein Teil von jener Kraft, die stets des Böse will und stets des Gute schafft.*" ("A part of this force which constantly wants evil and constantly does good.")

Was Mephisto at work in this family business?

Mephisto was also at times the subject of my conversations with Mme. H.: "Western mythology attributes an inaccurate role to the devil," she told me. "It considers him to be evil, bad in a powerful sense, whereas it is more accurate to see him as a trivial slanderer, expert in spreading dirty rumors everywhere, whose actions as a petty and fussy *little bourgeois* are carried forward by an eternal backbiting. To speak of a grandiose devil is a pure lie!"

Mme. H. who had recently studied German — by herself from books in order, as she claimed, to stretch her intellectual functions — rejoiced in being able to practice the language with me. She asked me to work with her on the Prologue in Heaven (*Prolog in Himmel*) from the beginning of *Faust*. Mephisto's assertions delighted her. "This is how Mr. G. sees the devil," she told me. "He is the one who incites, stimulates and serves as a goad. Without him man would fall asleep."

In fact, Mr. G. gave the devil an important role by including him in his main book of one thousand four hundred pages: *Beelzebub's Tales to His Grandson*.

I note here, my dear Richard, a few verses from the Prologue to Heaven, which Mme. H. particularly approved of:

> Mephisto to the Lord God:
> ... I have nothing to say about the sun and the spheres; all I can see is how men torment themselves. The little god of the world is still of the same caliber, as strange as on the first day. He would live I think more decently if you had struck his brain with a ray of celestial light. He calls this "reason" and only uses it to behave more savagely than animals...

> The Lord God to Mephisto:
> ... Here too you must present yourself frankly. I never hated your kind. Among all the spirits that deny, the spirit of cunning and malice displeases me the least of all. Man's activity too often slackens; he is prone to laziness and I like to see him with an active companion, one who excites him and can even create if necessary, like the devil...

An aspect of Mr. G.'s personality acted like this.

But make no mistake, my dear Richard, this Goethe-mania, widespread in Germany, does not exist in France. Goethe is known only to lovers of literature with a good general knowledge. Apart from students of German and their teachers, no one has read a single one of his works. He is known here only as a prominent German personality. This may seem strange to a German, even though a journalist like you would reject this kind of veneration of an individual. In fact, Goethe only impressed Mme. H. because his observations fell into one of the areas of thought expressed by Mr. G.

If you want to know what I think about it myself, here it is: The real devil, the force that is truly diabolical for relations between human beings, among other calamities, is ordinary habitual backbiting, the stupid and vulgar chatter that takes one or another person as its subject, a favorite pastime of idleness in thought and action. The real devil is slander, be it rambling or insidious.

I see myself obliged in this regard to build a monument to Mme. de S. I spoke a great deal with her in lively conversations that often took place when I drove her in the car. I participated for years in a group she led and met her several times in other contexts abroad. But I never, ever heard a single word of slander from her about anyone.

God knows however, how numerous and even violent were the oral and written attacks on Mr. G.'s teaching and his person, and on Mme. de S. Yet she never made any comment about their authors. On the contrary, I often heard her correct, in a noble and benevolent manner, pejorative judgments made by other people. I told her one day about someone who had been proposed for a certain task: "He's too stupid for that," I said.

"No, too good, too naive," she corrected me.

Although she emphasized the positive and favorable side of those who were spoken about in her presence, she could be quite severe when she was actually in front of them and could speak to them harshly. For instance, one of the well-to-do French women — a kind and pleasant person linked for a long time to Mme. de S. — showed a film one day that she had made herself about the Movements. It presented them in a false and unbearable way. Mme. de S. stood up in the middle of the film and exclaimed: "This is really shit!"

These words from the mouth of such a distinguished lady astounded us. Yet this apt expression kept the most hesitant among us from accepting things too easily.

Mme. de S. worked tirelessly to instill in everyone this rule of behavior: If your criticisms are justified, say them to the person's face, but never slander someone behind their back.

This extraordinary lady, for whom I continue to feel such great esteem and consideration, was unfortunately not close to my heart like Mr. G. or Mme. H. This was not deliberate on my part.

Regularly, methodically, the weekly group work carried out its task of education — or better, reeducation — using the knowledge received from practical and concrete experiences. Some results were achieved quickly while others took years. A human being is made for the highest achievement. That said, this does not happen by itself. To attain a certain level of evolution, only conscious development will bring results. In addition to this methodical work, the events and adventures experienced alongside Mr. G. produced surges of understanding, though not always immediately decipherable. This is why, my dear Richard, please do not regard what I am telling you as mere anecdotes, lest I miss my goal.

The example that a father, teacher, or master offers — through his own life — to a child, student, or disciple has an educational value. In this sense Mr. G. and Mme. de S. were living examples, not simply models. Woe to him who, concerned about his own development, tried to imitate one or the other of them. He would fall within himself between Charybdis and Scylla. Mme. de S. never attempted to imitate Mr. G. even remotely, either before or after his death. She directed this teaching according to her own way of being, and although the details gradually changed, the fundamental spirit of the "work" was maintained. And I am grateful to her.

The Movements, in which I later participated, constituted an important aspect of the teaching. They contributed to the transmission of the basis, the foundation, of this esoteric school — *esoteric* meaning simply that it leads to inner development. An esoteric school is in no way a pompous, pretentious or convoluted designation indicating mysterious gatherings, as people often imagine.

Our Movements classes took place on Saturday evenings in one of the large studios in the Salle Pleyel, where Ludolf also rented a studio. Mme. de S. led these classes assisted by a few specially-trained people. She had an extensive knowledge of dance. At ten years old, she was a young pupil in the corps de ballet of the Paris Opera and she directed, while still young, ballet troupes in various cities — in particular in Munich, where she met her husband Alexandre de S.

One day she related a revealing episode to the small circle of students who surrounded her: While still a child, between 1900 and 1904, she had danced alone in a large hall in Saint Petersburg in front of the Tsar and Tsarina. The Tsarina was charmed, brought her close and sent a minister to fetch a pretty ring adorned with a beautiful stone, which she offered her.

"I always kept this precious ring with pride," she recounted. "Later, my husband and I and our newborn child were forced to flee Russia with Mr. Gurdjieff across the Black Sea. When we arrived in Turkey, in Constantinople, we no longer had a penny, so my husband tried to sell the ring. But it had no value. The stone turned out to be fake. The absolute autocrat, the divinely revered Tsar and his powerful wife, had been brought from the treasury of the crown some worthless ring!" She added: "The Tsar's empire, where such corruption reigned, how could it not perish?"

The Movements, performed in a group, seemed very difficult to me at first. Slowly I became more adept at the precise gestures, often asymmetrical, which a trained attention had to sustain without wavering. Like the others, I was encouraged by Mme. de S.'s judicious and kind remarks; their meaning penetrated me directly, organically.

I cannot say much, my dear Richard, about the origin of these Movements, although I witnessed their creation on two occasions. Mr. G. led the class himself and Mme. de S., a talented pianist, accompanied him on the piano. It was in fact the old Mr. G. himself, inspired, who demonstrated the exercises with great skill. The students in the front rows, more able and experienced, immediately performed the exercises more or less well, followed by those in the back rows. Mr. G. then crossed the room, examined the whole ensemble, came back to the front and changed or clarified the Movements he had just created, indicating with a few key words the general choreographic layout of the class. Then the dance took shape.

We often started in a circle and Mr. G. would take one of the students by the hand and dance with her, in the circle or across the rows, without ever jostling anyone. A perfect sense of harmony seemed to guide the gestures of this old man, whose flexibility and unexpected grace, mixed with the beautiful and rhythmic music, deeply delighted us. A certain disorder quickly reigned in the back rows but we were transported, no one minded, and the expression on Mme. de S.'s face, usually so sober, radiated a mysterious joy. The Saturday classes where we learned to correct ourselves and refine our attention were quite different.

Marthe de Gaigneron transcribed these Movements in a special symbolic language over the course of many years. These notes are still used today and provide the basis for the numerous films made on the subject.

In the countryside my in-laws invited their close and distant relatives, friends and acquaintances to the castle during the summer of 1948. How can I describe these wholesale and retail bakers, charcutiers and butchers, these taxi drivers and shopkeepers of all kinds, to which were added movie people, as well as talkative and voracious Parisian rascals who spent two weeks on the property? They were the admiring audience necessary for the success of my in-laws. I had learned in the group to make full use of everything, so I took an interest, adopting a positive attitude in this world that I did not know, which was for my own good too.

During this stay, Marie-Claude — my little three-year-old daughter, with her bushy, curly hair that was always messy — hid all day with her dolls under an enormous table in the dining room. Moreover, if my brother-in-law, her uncle, arrived with his big beard, she would refuse to move and would scream if anyone tried to make her leave her hiding place.

Marie-Claude had gotten into the habit of standing in front of a tall mirror in the hall, making faces and then laughing very hard, banging her head against this two-meter-high mirror.

Amused, we let her do it. I was far less amused however, when a workman ran up to me one day where I was working far from the castle, and stammered breathlessly: "Sir, your daughter split her head."

Apparently I was no longer an invalid, for I darted like an arrow across the fields. My wife held the little one in her arms, covered with blood. Next to my wife, my six-year-old son Jean-Pierre on his knees prayed out loud with great intensity yet without crying. I don't know what upset me more, anxiety for her or tenderness for him.

Doctor Roth arrived quickly from Chinon. Noting only a few cuts in her scalp, he shaved her head and then sewed up the wounds amid her cries and screams. A thousand shards were all that remained of the heavy mirror that had fallen on the little girl's head.

Doctor Roth, a Romanian Jew, had been deported to Buchenwald and returned alone; his parents, first wife, and two children were killed by the Germans. A few occasions had brought us together. He was my family's doctor and we had become friends. He came to see me from time to time when his schedule permitted. This man was an excellent physician whom all of Chinon and its surroundings esteemed; he was considerate and kind, and he went out of his way without complaint at any hour of the day or night to rush to see a sick person, even if far away.

He had been remarried for two years when, sometime after the incident of the mirror, he lost his only son, aged one. He felt pursued by fate and became inconsolable. He came to see me almost every day, since I was the only friend with whom he could confide the horrors he had experienced in the extermination camp and feel some relief from the wounds that still burned.

Filled with compassion, I spoke with him about Mr. G's "work" ideas. For several days he listened with great interest, asking intelligent and appropriate questions which showed his sensitivity and kindness. Then his medical practice kept him away for a week. On his next visit, looking me straight in the eye, he said: "If your master can bring back my little child who recently died, I could believe in him and in what you told me."

I was speechless. Completely rational and rather Cartesian, Doctor Roth had never seemed illogical or lacking in reason. I tried to guide him back to more sensible and healthy feelings but in vain. He persisted in his crazy request, and I had to withdraw cautiously in order not to give him false hope.

It was a good lesson for me. What do we know about what goes on in the depths of a person's psyche?

My brother Fritz came from the United States that summer. The castle excited him, of course, and even more so the orchards and the giant apples I had kept to impress him. We teased each other: "I have never seen such huge apples in America," he told me.

"But there are no skyscrapers so high in Europe," I retorted.

His quarrel with our father worried and weighed on me and I tried hard to bring them closer together, but this too was in vain. Their quarrel had more to do with resentment than a simple disagreement, and they remained in their respective positions.

Fritz was delighted to find me recovered and out of the dark depressive state which to my surprise he had previously observed in Paris, although he had not said a word to me about it. So I spoke to him about the cause of my recovery, the extraordinary nourishment that I had received through the teaching of Mr. G., using the Viennese dialect. Fritz and I had always exchanged frankly, and we understood each other in the language of our past intimacy.

He showed no interest in participating in the self-development I proposed to him. He was more interested in the great athletic activities of which he was and still is so capable. His refusal, however, took a very strange form to my ears when he said: *"I am an agnostic."*

He repeated this statement several times in English.

One Saturday morning, we decided to sail to London to see our sister. No sooner said than done! My brother-in-law wanted us to bring his sports car to Paris, so we drove it there. I didn't have a passport but the director of the cinema, the famous Mr. Villiers, who was always up to all sorts of tricks, found a way to get me one in two hours — on a summer Saturday afternoon when all administrative offices were closed and without my having to show any papers. One would have concluded that he cultivated his "friendships" even in the secret services of the police. My brother Fritz was amazed: "This would be impossible in the United States."

"Even in the land of unlimited possibilities!" I retorted.

We had a moving and affectionate reunion with my sister Hanna, whom we saw for the first time since our scattered departures from Vienna. She liked London and spoke a great deal about the war and the destruction of the city as she walked everywhere with us. We were truly happy. My brother never stopped telling Viennese jokes in English, each funnier than the last. I can't resist, Richard, the pleasure of giving you an example that made me laugh: Fritz asked for a beer in a pub and was served dishwater, bitter and lukewarm. He tasted it and asked the bartender with a perfectly serious face: "Who died in there?"

Like my brother, my sister did not welcome hearing about Mr. G.'s teaching. Was it due to my clumsiness? In those days I was trying to convey what was so precious about it to those closest to me. But sadly without success.

Hanna's opposition grew when she came to Paris. At that time, I had a lot of interaction with Mrs. March, whom you knew so well, Richard. Mr. G. named this already old student, originally from Frankfurt: "Sausage", or in French, "Saucisse de Francfort." I introduced her to my sister and showed them Paris. Hanna was happy and enthusiastic.

Deciding to attend lunch at Mr. G.'s with Mrs. March around one o'clock, I suggested to Hanna that we have a short period of separation, but Mrs. March intervened: "You're not going to leave your sister alone when she comes to see you for the first time! I'm taking her with me to Mr. G. At least she'll see something interesting."

Mrs. March did not listen to my reservations or my fears, confident in herself and in the curiosity that she had aroused in my sister. My apprehensions, alas, were only too well-justified. Dear Hanna — frightened, intimidated — despite the kind attentions of Mme. de S., was in no way prepared for such a meeting. She had not asked for it and did not know what to do or how to behave. She left in a gloomy mood, having understood nothing, and showered me with reproaches. Why hadn't I let her go to the Louvre? She returned to London in this state. Mme. de S. also blamed me. As for Sausage, wisdom dictated that nothing be blamed on her. The slightest observation always led to endless complications.

When Mrs. March went to Vienna, where she knew no one, I gave her out of kindness the address of my father, who had recently returned from the United States. Sometime later very upset, he reprimanded me to no end: "Why did you send me this Prussian bitch, so authoritarian and demanding? Do you really want to torment me in my old age?"

He forgave me with difficulty.

My attempts to make others understand what was so dear and precious to me and thereby help them were not all in vain, however. Mme. H. proposed the following exercise to the members of her group: choose a person you know but if possible not a relative, and carefully lead the conversation toward the ideas of the work without attaching importance to the result of this exchange but rather to observations about yourself.

The first difficulty was finding an ear for my experiment. In Chinon I saw only my family, the agricultural workers, a few mechanics and shopkeepers. In Paris, only the wholesalers at Les Halles and my group companions. Whom to choose?

The wall which enclosed the farthest orchards from the castle touched the garden of a small property belonging to a certain Bertaux family. Mr. Lavenne, my head of production, having had trouble with these people, insisted that I intervene and tell them of my dissatisfaction. They had, in fact, employed our workers for a few days without asking, and we did not want our workers to be used as reserve for occasional work elsewhere, especially in the high season.

I paid my first visit to the Bertaux family and was received very kindly by a man of about thirty-five named Jacques. A professional singer with an open face, he knew nothing of the tale about our workers. He summoned his old father, his short and plump mother, his wife and the sixteen-year-old son from her first marriage. Very happy to get to know their neighbor, they did not let me open my mouth but spoke at length about their lives. They were rich shipowners from Dunkerque who had been driven to ruin and moved to Touraine at the start of the war.

A simple and good neighborly relationship was then established with Jacques Bertaux. He came to see me from time to time and I often lent him my tools. One day he sang and pleasantly surprised me with his beautiful, well-developed bass voice. I decided to use him for my exercise and little by little tilted our conversations toward the desired themes. Soon our lively discussions focused on art and philosophy. I became more and more keenly interested in this experience, as did my group companions, to whom I communicated my observations each week. Everyone already knew Bertaux without having seen him.

Finally, the time came to talk to him directly about Mr. G.'s teaching. He asked for clarification, wanted to know more. I told him of the upcoming visit of a person more competent than I whom he could meet. Due to their isolation and solitude from 1940 to 1948 of which they were only now becoming aware, the Bertaux family seemed happier with our relationship than with the ideas I presented to them. But in Jacques, the ideas seemed to be making headway.

It had long been decided that the whole group would come to Chinon for six days in the spring of 1948. With the exception of Ludolf, who was very ill and to my great regret had to stay in Paris with Jacqueline, all the members of the group came: Nadia; Étienne with his big black beard; Jean and Claude, our two invalids, the latter accompanied by his wife Suzanne, so devoted to serving him; another Jean, my friend still to this day; a Jew hiding with Mme. H. during the war; and others.

Upon their rather amusing arrival at the Chinon station, I took Mme. H. in my big car along with the oldest and most disabled. The others climbed into a large trailer pulled by a tractor for five kilometers of wandering at low speed across Touraine, which was in full bloom. We gathered together for a group meeting every evening. Some people wanted to work in the fields or orchards during the day, which made my workers smile and made their job more difficult.

Jacques Bertaux met Mme. H. on the second day, in my presence at the beginning. He told her more about his life than he had told me and declared himself keenly interested in the ideas I had presented to him. Mme. H. admitted to him very frankly with a smile for me: "That you are now here is the result of an exercise, the real goal of which was different."

His wife also came, and on the last two days they both participated in our meetings.

This young couple, the Bertaux, moved to Paris sometime later with their son, who was able to return to school. Jacques attempted to resume his singing career along with other professional activities, happy to have emerged from his wartime lethargy. He became a very active member of Mme. H.'s new group, and we remained friends for a long time before the whirlwinds of Paris separated us.

For you, my dear Richard, I can happily mention other aspects likely to help you better understand the person of Mr. G. and his influence. However, a good translation, apart from a few mistakes, of Kathryn Hulme's book *Undiscovered Country* appeared in 1968 in Germany published by Herder. Try to find this work, as it gives authentic and important insights into the man Gurdjieff and his activities. The French edition, published under the inadequate title *Ma Conversion*, is a total failure.

To use an analogy that is familiar to you, I would say that Mr. G. was like a large force field or, similar to a transformer, a source of high voltage. In his presence a powerful force appeared. Anyone who operated on low voltage in their daily life and then connected directly to this high voltage, risked breakdowns or accidents. This is why those who brought seekers to this esoteric school absolutely had to show caution and the ability to choose, at the risk of generating more harm than good, the least of the possible evils being total incomprehension.

Outside his apartment Mr. G. moved about as if masked. I often took him by car to various stores, hammams, or elsewhere. Uninformed people, employees or passers-by, noticed this man who was not quite like the others and spontaneously adopted an attitude of respect.

Mr. G. himself always tried even at home to camouflage or diminish this impression. To fall before him in a sort of interior exaltation, externally perceptible though infrequent, evoked an observation like: "If explosion in you, then plunge behind in cold water for a long time. I'm only here for regular work, not for excitement."

Or: "Do you know what the next degree is after fullness? Blast. So don't overfill yourself!"

I remain convinced that no one has ever understood the multiple aspects of this man. Sometimes he deceived one or another person by playing tricks on them, like the mischievous Till[1], but his tricks touched inner levels very deeply.

He particularly loved children, and when they attended lunch, he gave them places of honor and devoted himself to them. The little ones quickly lost all shyness. Between them and the old man, conversations took place that were very moving, rich with wisdom and reflections.

---

[1] Till Eulenspiegel (Mischievious Till) was a folk hero in the German tradition, dating from the 16th century.

Chapter X
THE FOURTH WAY

René Daumal was a friend of Mme. de S.'s son-in-law Philippe and not yet known as an eminent poet as he is today. He died in 1943 of tuberculosis. Daumal was open about the radical turning point of his meeting with Mr. G. which transformed his poetry and allowed it to emerge into its true expression. *Mount Analogue*, which you know and for which there is a German translation, is a symbolic description of the work of Mr. G., as well as an expression of gratitude to Alexandre de S., the husband of Mme. de S., although Daumal's work remains an enigma for those who are not familiar with Gurdjieff.

As I mentioned previously, Alexandre de S. and his wife met in Germany. She was a member of the Dalcroze dance school in Dresden before the war and a professional dancer. He worked as a theater designer at the Residenztheater in Munich. A Georgian from Tiflis, he had become deeply imbued with German culture. I translated many of her husband's texts for Mme. de S. relating to a new stage lighting technique to which she still held the rights. I sweated a lot on the theater terms that I didn't know in either German or French.

At the beginning of 1939, when the risk of war was becoming clearer in Europe, Mr. G. returned to Paris — because, so he said, in a period rich in conflicts, his ideas and convictions had more chance of penetrating people's mentality, thought and feeling. This is indeed what happened, beyond all expectations.

Today, P. D. Ouspensky's book *In Search of the Miraculous* brings to the great benefit of readers the work of the first group in Moscow between 1915 and 1921-22. To date there is no equally exhaustive and authentic account about the Parisian group from 1939 to 1946. However, this period was even more intense than that of the First World War and the Russian revolution. It seems to me that this work in Paris during the Second World War, because it was less accompanied by intellectual explanations, took the life experiences of G.'s students more into account, first and foremost.

Mme. H. spoke with me a great deal about the work with Mr. G. in Paris during these war years. Recently, a television interview with Pierre Schäffer shed further light on this period, describing a special atmosphere. Other students have passed on their experiences orally as well.

Mr. G. would have said: "In this group at this period, I wrote the third series of my works in a living way."

Many of these companions who rightfully acquired the title of elders, are no longer with us.

When the German army invaded France in May and June of 1940, the population in the north of the country and the Paris region fled before them. Mme. de S. departed by herself, loaded with two enormous suitcases containing all of Mr. G.'s writings, which she placed in a safe location. The circumstances of the exodus were chaotic. Without her courageous act there would be no written legacy of Mr. G. today. As she told me later, he had systematically trained her to develop courage, especially in Germany during the unrest of 1921-22 that followed the First World War when he taught her how to dodge the soldiers' bullets.

Going back a bit further, my dear Richard, I will explain how and why Mr. G. came to Berlin after World War One and subsequently left Germany.

In 1920, he fled Russia and went to Constantinople with a few of his students, including Jeanne and Alexandre de S. He adopted a political attitude of strict neutrality, completely convinced that human beings live without any common sense. When I knew him even later, he rarely offered value judgments regarding political circumstances, neither for nor against the Soviet system or Hitler.

He did say, however, that the inner work he proposed, more

or less adapted to the Russian mentality, would be "impossible" in a totalitarian state. In the authoritarian empire of the Tsar, Mr. G. had managed to overcome many difficulties, but he believed that the rise of Russian communism would lead to the spiritual death of the country for a long time, despite his confidence in the religious spirit deeply rooted in the Russian people. In any case, after the revolution of 1917, the "work" could not be carried out in Russia. While this assessment may seem obvious today, it was not so clear in 1918. Yet Mr. G. stated it without the slightest doubt, foreshadowing what he sensed also in Berlin in 1922.

If Mr. G. spoke out against any political phenomenon, it was against the "British imperialism" that he had personally confronted during the Anglo-Tibetan war. He sometimes expressed his regret that the peaceful Tibetan people had been so violently occupied by the English military, for no valid reason. In his great work *Beelzebub's Tales,* he expressed this view by describing "the degrees of human infamy:

1. Violence and ordinary infamy
2. Major crimes
3. (He took a deep breath), *"English power politics"*

Mr. G.'s participation in fighting alongside the Tibetans against the English justified this judgment, but with the consequence that he was now included on a British Intelligence Service blacklist. Later, when attempting to enter England, this gave him great difficulties. The intervention of Captain Bennett, who was a member of the Intelligence Service and had met Mr. G. in Constantinople, was required to overcome these obstacles, but only for very short stays.

After leaving Russia, as I mentioned, Mr. G. went to Constantinople. But the rapid growth of Mustapha Kemal Pasha's Turkish national movement heralded troubled times. P. D. Ouspensky advised Mr. G. to emigrate to Germany, preferably Berlin, arguing in favor of the high German culture eminent in Europe, and assuming that after the sufferings and disappointments of the First World War, people in Germany would be more open to his ideas than in other places. After the publication of *Tertium Organum*, Ouspensky had established close relationships in London that he willingly placed at the disposal of his master, but he considered with some reservation that Berlin would be a more suitable place than London — which in any case turned out to be forbidden to Mr. G. for any long stays, as explained above.

While Mr. G. had traveled a great deal in the Middle East and Asia and spoke many Middle Eastern languages and dialects, he had never been in contact with a Western country other than Russia — although Moscow was not a perfect example of European culture. Thus, he listened to the opinions of those around him who knew Europe and were keen on Western European culture.

At the time, no one mentioned France as a place to settle, even though Alexandre de S.'s wife was French. As Mr. G. wrote: "France was considered the country of champagne, of frivolous women, of French cancan, the privileged place of pleasure of the Russian grand dukes." Later he discovered for himself that the Paris of foreign visitors had nothing to do with the real France.

Mr. G. therefore arrived in Berlin during the political unrest of the years of crisis that followed the First World War. He settled there rather poorly with a few students. By "rather poorly," I mean what an emigrant easily understands: an abundant lack of money. He tried to attract attention to his ideas through writings and conferences. Soon regular meetings brought some people together but without real group work yet being offered.

Much later, in 1964, Mme. de S. gave me some of Mr. G.'s writings from this period that had been translated into German as well as several articles about him that had been written by others. I am convinced that she did this to make me aware of certain aspects of his stay in Berlin and thereby prepare me for the difficulties I would face later in my own German endeavor.

When I read this material, the clarity and sober tone of Mr. G.'s writing made an impression on me, but most of the other articles horrified me. These writings advocated, in a way that made my hair stand on end, a pathetic occultism, hackneyed and trivial, a continuation of the thousand-year-old Germanic empire for which "Herr Gurdjieff" had the necessary material at the ready. I doubt that any of his experienced students who read these writings had any real command of the German language or any control over these publications; otherwise none of this abject nonsense would have seen the light of day. Alexandre de S. however spoke German well. Were these works published without his knowledge or perhaps in his absence?

Mr. G. soon noticed that something was wrong in the meetings in Berlin. An unhealthy mentality thwarted his attempts with the people in these groups. They adopted behaviors contrary to his ideas — in fact, totally inappropriate and troubling attitudes. Mme. de Mangoldt's aversion to Mr. G. dated from this time, when she heard about the meetings in Berlin. You certainly remember, Richard, the sharp and often repeated assertion of the extraordinary lady who was head of a publishing house esteemed throughout the world: "Ouspensky, yes; Gurdjieff, no."

Mme. de Mangoldt was impressed by Ouspensky's *In Search of the Miraculous* which she published with enthusiasm, and over long evenings she questioned me about its contents. This book, as everyone knows, talks only about Gurdjieff and his ideas.

The nationalist core — the spiritual background of Berlin and the country in general — displeased Mr. G. so strongly that he began looking for another land of asylum. He went to England several times to meet Ouspensky for this purpose, each time crossing France by train. This is how, as he recounts in *Beelzebub's Tales* in the chapter on France, he discovered this country and its inhabitants and appreciated them for himself.

At last, in 1922 he made the Château du Prieuré in Fontainebleau his permanent residence and that of his family, as well as the place where his Russian, American and English students could come for extended visits. No French people were there at that time except Mme. de S. There were rumors about the death of Katherine Mansfield, whose grave is located in Fontainebleau-Avon cemetery, four or five meters from those of

Mr. G., his wife and his mother. This man's compassion for the dying Katherine was abundantly repaid with slander and backbiting about which Ouspensky has already spoken.

You may be wondering, my dear Richard, why does François Grunwald write all this, which has already been published in various works that are easily accessible? French people, friends and non-friends, may judge this information as useless, superfluous, even harmful. The answer is: It is enough for me to see in this a meaning for myself and for you, my friend Richard.

Another attempt to spread the valuable ideas of Mr. G. in Germany came about in 1963 when with Richard Dill, I tried to make them known to a number of people who were looking for them. It was necessary for these people to be aware of these ideas before taking up serious work. So we formed groups and translated books. It was not easy, but the foundation was laid. Whether for a hut or a cathedral, that is a big question.

You know only too well how things turned out. We got our hands dirty while developing this group. We went through mud and rain. Possibly my faults and mistakes played a major role. That a doctor, not exactly stupid, but a little narrow-minded opened a shop for his own interests is not original but really not the most important. There are many such ventures all over the world which inevitably end in a miserable fiasco. My friendship with Michel P. offered a new opportunity later, with the result that he was able to build on our early foundation, if not a cathedral, at least a habitable house.

Mrs. March had long before me dabbled in this effort to bring Mr. G's ideas to Germany. By herself she had translated the one thousand four hundred pages of *Beelzebub* and, with Count Arnold von Keyserling, Ouspensky's *In Search of the Miraculous*. In the summer of 1949, in my presence Mr. G. entrusted to Keyserling the responsibility of translating his works into German thus charging him to spread his ideas, assigning Mrs. March and me – the beginner – to help.

The mark of Count Keyserling is evident in the excellent style of the translation of *In Search*. The mistakes in the first edition should not be blamed on him even though correcting them was a lot of work for me. Keyserling was not familiar enough with the ideas of Mr. G. nor experienced enough in this way. But it happened that Mrs. March managed so well – this is no slander – that Keyserling became disgusted with the project and abandoned it. Despite my esteem and sympathy for him and his wife, I could do nothing about it. Too bad. What followed was a disaster, a mountain of troubles that you are familiar with: a German *Beelzebub* so quirky that no one could make head or tails of it, a failed mess.

And us? When the wine is poured it must be drunk. Do not think I am irritated by all these things that occupied us so completely. You would be mistaken. Even then they did not exasperate me. I remained free inside. Failures of whatever degree are merely signs of human weakness rather than deliberate villainy, which is extremely rare.

I write down what I lived through and experienced as accurately as I can so you can draw your own conclusions and perhaps change your inner attitude. My dear friend, if you are constantly exasperated, as you tell me you are, by a new outbreak of Nazism in your country, we cannot progress together. This possibility is very unpleasant, but it is a fact and it is something over which neither you nor I have the slightest control. I do not want to waste the little time and energy that I have left fighting against windmills. I believe this approach would be insane. And as for your constant exasperation, which is sometimes explosive, you answer me: "This is precisely the German character. This is how I am!"

I do not accept this answer because it takes away any hope in the effort of trying to bring about change.

Anti-semitic Jews and Germans who hate Germans — like Nietzsche, for example — are suspect to me. If you are ready to work on your inner development with the same sincerity and force that you feel when you get exasperated about this or that, then I am ready to try again, as much as my aging strength permits and if I may be allowed to do so. Without you, none of this interests me. With you, it interests me only if you learn to use your sincere emotions as signals. Inner disturbances such as these are merely signs pointing to something real. This means first of all that under no circumstances should they be pushed back or repressed by an upside-down training, turning you into a moron or indifferent person who takes himself as someone of impassioned wisdom. This twisted model serves as an ideal for many candidates in spirituality who unfortunately sometimes achieve that ideal to the detriment of their overall development.

The perpetual changes in our negative emotions (like fear, guilt, desire for revenge, malicious joy, etc.) or in excessive emotions (like feverishness, excitement, vanity, enthusiasm, etc.) have only indicative value. This is their justification. They are a thermometer. Wanting to immediately change the air or water temperature itself is *quixotic*. But dressing more warmly, or not getting into water that is too cold or too hot, is another matter.

If we do not learn to see these emotions and to consider them as meaningful indications, the path to true feeling will remain closed. True feelings are never negative, nor excessive, nor even transitory. They are, whatever their taste, whole, joyful, like on the Cross. Most human beings never experience such true feelings, so totally pure and full, which is a pity. One must reach higher for true feelings, often with effort. Or if they are given to us at times, we must recognize and appreciate them and work to come back to them or prepare for their return. It is just as difficult to explain the color red to a blind man as it is to explain the difference between pleasure and bliss to one who is misguided.

One day I was the amazed and admiring witness to the masterful way in which Mr. G., visibly angry, thundered against someone. Another person had justifiably angered him but he transferred that anger to the first person, who was totally innocent but for whom this treatment proved very useful. It was literally a transfer of energy from one person, for whom it was no longer worthwhile to another person, for whom it was a great help. This attitude, already closer to art than work, could serve as a model of self-control yet would probably be impossible to imitate.

What I am proposing to you was also valid for Mr. G. himself, who certainly did not emerge from limbo accomplished or already perfected. Thus his hero Beelzebub, the personification of himself, got carried away and tried to take up a cause about the order of the universe that did not concern him. Yet he did not want to accept being denied this possibility so he rebelled. In consequence, God the Father banished him to our solar system. Beelzebub thus came to know planet Earth. The story of Beelzebub's rehabilitation is, as you know, of luminous and striking beauty.

And now, let's get to work! No effort is wasted when we fight against our leaden, harmful, and more or less fatal tendencies. Sooner or later an effort yields its value and its dividends. The hopeless idiot who accomplishes the effort also receives his share of the benefit. The real work is this struggle against gravity, against the implacable and natural inclination toward shadow by the no less natural, and often more fragile, taste of light.

This is structured work. First of all, it is about strengthening our power of discrimination, our ability to see and feel what is what. Perhaps you have already taken this step, since a keener eye is needed when we wish to observe something finer. The next step could be called "the proper use of discrimination." This skill must be astutely applied, lest the qualities or results already obtained be lost in the sands of waking sleep.

Do you really believe that the laws of creation, maintenance and destruction of the world are accessible to ordinary human understanding and appreciation? If that were the case, a recipe book would suffice. But this is not so. The study and exploration of these laws requires a special understanding, intelligence of the heart and power of adaptation. Mr. G. tried to help us in that direction.

Chapter XI
IN MEMORY OF...

Here are a few pages, my dear Richard, that I dedicate to the memory of some of the students of Mr. G. who were close to me.

PIERRE ABOULKER

Between 1955 and 1956 my medical studies were almost complete. I was thirty-eight years old with four children, and twelve to fourteen years older than my fellow students. Exams followed one after another. However, my responsibilities at the hospital were holding me back from classes and I never attended a lecture.

One afternoon when I had devoted myself to administrative tasks and found they had taken less time than expected, I made my way to the medical and surgical pathology course because I had heard good things about it. I had to overcome my gloom however, when the subject was announced: "prostatic adenomas," the height of boredom. I climbed to the top of the amphitheater and sat at the back with my notebook.

But the speaker, Pierre Aboulker, caught my attention. He walked around the room in an authoritative way speaking in a captivating manner on a thankless subject. Sometime later on an announcement board at Cochin Hospital, I noticed this message: "Professor Pierre Aboulker is looking for students for an experiment."

I applied, even though my specialization kept me in the psychiatric hospital every day. Aboulker took an interest in my relatively older age and my specialization in psychiatry and invited me to come to his department twice a week to study the effects of certain treatments. This went on for a year, and a warm rapport developed between us — he at the top of the medical hierarchy, and I still a student at the bottom. Medical careers depend on mentors, but I expected nothing from him for my future in psychiatry. This made our relationship freer and lighter.

When the year was over he asked me to stay in his department to work there twice a week, this time as a psychiatrist, together with one of his colleagues. "The time has come to focus on the clinical exploration and application of psychosomatic medicine," he told us. "A lot of theoretical data is published, but nothing is studied on a practical level."

Starting out as a Jewish medical student from Algiers, Aboulker had risen to become a urological surgeon at the highest level of the Parisian medical hierarchy. As an Algerian Jew he was an extremely rare exception.

He was also a pioneer of medical psychology in France. He became a leader of this discipline and the founding president of the Psychosomatic Society, which he invited us to join. It met twice a month. He then proposed a challenging program to us: the fascinating and unique study of the psychological and sexual implications of urology.

There are a thousand things to say about this subject, and soon we published some of our observations in medical journals. Thus we established the first psychosomatic medicine consultation available to students. However, most of the medical and surgical assistants did not hide their indifference to these new views about psychosomatic medicine. Doctors and nursing staff were only concerned with scientific considerations, instrument technique, instructions to follow. They found it unacceptable that anyone would poke their nose into relationships with patients or medical staff. Our position continued only thanks to the unwavering protection of Aboulker.

After a presentation by Professor Aboulker in front of all the staff on duty proving that the death of a certain patient was due among other things to a conflict between doctors, their indifference turned to hostility, and more and more of the medical staff began to resent us. At the same time my relationship with

Aboulker grew closer. We often stayed together for a long time after his Monday consultation. He expressed his dismay at the total psychological ignorance of doctors in general and more particularly of surgeons. He sometimes placed his hands on my shoulders during his consultation, in a heavy gesture of despair: "Will we ever manage to be done with these Augean stables?" he said. "The man I spoke of that day was operated on unnecessarily five times, when in fact his case falls under the psychiatric domain. It is inhuman. What's more, it is ruinous."

Around 1969 Mrs. Nott, a former student of Mr. G. from the Fontainebleau era, gave a piano recital in Paris. During the intermission, I saw Professor Aboulker talking very animatedly with Mme. de S. and a few others. Then he came toward me: "So you are part of it too," he said to me. "Did you know Mr. G.?" And passing his hand over his forehead, he continued, "I must have been blind not to have guessed it before now."

I realized that it was Aboulker whom Mr. G. held in high regard and called "the doctor" in the reports that I sometimes read of the "work" during wartime! I had never met him in Mr. G.'s apartment between 1946 and 1949 as he was often away outside Paris.

Companions from his former group who loved and esteemed Professor Aboulker understood that his sense of compassion and his exceptional intelligence had earned him a privileged relationship with Mr. G. Mme. H. confirmed this to me. After saying something important, Mr. G. often turned to Pierre Aboulker: "What do you think, doctor?" And Aboulker always responded with tact and modesty.

We talked a great deal about our experiences with Mr. G. during the long intermission, though we did not return to the subject for quite a while. Aboulker told me: "It was a beautiful time, even though everyone around me suffered. It was war. Because I was Jewish, I was able to continue working at the hospital on the condition of remaining in the shadows. I had plenty of time. I traveled by bicycle through Paris and even did some hiking. Since then, I've been chasing time. Eternally in a hurry, I live with such a permanent impression of lacking time that I have difficulty devoting any to myself. Mr. G. will remain unforgettable for me. Although I am now going my own way, it is a way that he discovered and made possible."

From that day on, our privileged relationship in medical practice became more distant. Aboulker likely feared that any indiscretion on my part would bring him additional difficulties. The laborious introduction of psychosomatics into a surgical department had already caused enough problems for him with his staff. One can imagine that they would have abandoned him entirely if his esoteric aspirations had come to light. Such interests are not well thought of in Parisian society. Over time he and I again found a good rapport, but never as it was at the beginning.

In 1964 Pierre Aboulker was appointed to a chaired professorship. It was an important and unexpected honor as there was only one medical faculty in Paris. This was a new chair of urology created just for him and ended up raising many questions stemming from jealousy or curiosity. His solemn inaugural lecture brought together the university authorities and all of Paris, as well as the most senior members of the Gurdjieff groups. It was certainly the first time in Paris that the inauguration of a new chair in surgery was so strongly tinged with spirituality. So much so that during the private reception that followed, Professor Henri Mondor, a great surgeon, writer and member of the French Academy, said: "Aboulker! You should have become a bishop or rather, a great rabbi!" This short, pleasant soundbite of Parisian life amidst toasts of champagne aroused general laughter.

Two months later, the secret behind his appointment was revealed. One Monday in April of 1964, Aboulker ordered all the personnel in his department to be present the following Friday, except those whom, according to rumors, the police were sending to the provinces. On Friday, having barely crossed the numerous cordons of police, I learned the reason: "We are operating on de Gaulle," went the rumor.

Around 10:00 a.m., Professor Aboulker left the operating room accompanied by his first assistant Professor Steg and the anesthetist Professor Lassner, a good friend of mine from Vienna. All three were smiling and Aboulker seemed relieved. He had just removed a benign adenoma from our famous president's prostate. In an aside to me, he commented: "In the event of complications, I would have had indescribable troubles. There were only Jews around him!"

At noon, when I went out I saw special editions of the newspapers carrying the story. On the front page there was a rather old photo of Professor Aboulker surrounded by his team members. In a corner at the top I recognized my own face, barely visible.

Shortly afterward the same afternoon, I discovered that the head of state had a number of enemies in intellectual circles. Doctors whose hostility towards de Gaulle surpassed their medical knowledge called me and asked: "You might as well tell me. Was it prostate cancer?"

"Since when is prostate cancer operated on?" I replied.

An awkward silence followed, their embarrassment at being instructed in surgery by a psychiatrist and their realization that they had just exposed their wish to see de Gaulle disappear from the political scene.

In the following days, de Gaulle's presence dominated the hospital. I accompanied Aboulker and his team during a few visits to the illustrious patient. Upon entering the large room, Aboulker was greeted with the words: "How are you, professor?"

There was no point in asking de Gaulle the same question! One day when Aboulker wanted to remove a bandage, de Gaulle tried to help him. But the surgeon replied: "Let yourself be taken care of General, at least for once!"

The rest of us who were outside, laughed: "Wasn't that a historic moment?"

I provided psychosomatic consultation in Professor Aboulker's department until 1976, although our relationship changed after 1970. Both of us had been touched by Indian spirituality. We met once or twice a year to pay our respects to a wise man from India who had been invited to France and had long discussions there.

Professor Aboulker died suddenly in June 1976 at Orly airport on his way to a conference in Athens. I truly enjoyed my exchanges with this extraordinary man who taught me so much.

JEAN VAYSSE

Jean Vaysse, one of my closest group companions, was also a surgeon, with a handsome, virile appearance that could not be missed. Joining the group after the death of Mr. G., he was an active member, beside and under the direction of Mme. de S. A solid friendship developed between him, a young but experienced doctor and me, an older but novice one.

Vaysse was a born surgeon, infinitely skilled, and one of the first to perform open heart surgery alongside a famous cardiac surgeon. Unlike me, a latecomer to medicine, he had pursued his life and career at full speed, constantly ahead in everything and while still young, operating on his colleagues and their relatives. These services between doctors were provided free of charge. Thus he lived modestly and for a long time in cramped conditions with his family of four children.

From dawn to dusk Vaysse displayed a constant, extraordinary energy for work that I have never encountered in anyone else. Tirelessly active without ever losing his calm, he operated every day, taught at the university or at the hospital, worked with Mme. de S. and led groups. We used to meet once a month late in the evening in a bar near the Champs-Elysées for what was for both of us a friendly and valuable exchange.

Some of his listeners could not bear his rhetorical lecture style with its well-defined, intellectual purpose. Spontaneous and friendly in private, Vaysse functioned in public like an intellectual machine. He retained from his study of psychology only the logical aspects, forgetting the psyche. He was sometimes surprised to have to submit, openly and sincerely, to arguments of a strictly psychological nature.

When I finally opened my medical practice, Vaysse gave me considerable help. I sent him all my surgical patients and they came back grateful, having fallen under his spell. For example, there was a married couple who were anthroposophists[1] and refused to agree to surgery for the husband's cancer. I managed to persuade them to consult "my" surgeon. After the operation, the man told me: "Being operated on by such a surgeon is almost a pleasure."

I generally assisted Vaysse during my patients' operations. Step by step he explained his gestures and actions, always with calm and skill. One day I was delayed and came at the end of the afternoon to visit an eighty-year-old woman whose breast he had operated on earlier in the day. The elderly woman was seated in her room eating her evening meal with her right hand. Annoyed, I asked the nurse why Professor Vaysse had not operated on my patient that day. "I was present myself when he removed her right breast," she replied.

It was incredible! I witnessed similar events countless times including in my own family. Previously, when my son Jean-Pierre underwent a small operation in Chinon, he remained in bed for eight days. When Vaysse operated on Sylvain however, he was playing ball two hours later in the garden. Richard, I am not exaggerating!

Sometimes I joined Vaysse during his vacations in Royan on the Atlantic. One day, when I arrived he had just come out of the water. He told me that it had taken him three hours that afternoon to save his wife, who had fallen from her small sailboat into the waves of a turbulent sea. Neither of them showed the slightest disturbance.

He once asked me to attend one of the Gurdjieff groups he was leading because the attitude of a certain young woman worried him. She sat almost in a trance with her hypnotized eyes fixed on Jean, who was speaking in a compelling manner. Later I saw her in my medical office. A prolonged interview with this perfectly normal person, recently divorced, revealed that she had without realizing it fallen deeply in love with her instructor. "I

---

[1] A formal educational, therapeutic and creative system established by Rudolf Steiner seeking to use mainly natural means to optimize physical and mental health and well-being.

am sitting in front of him in true ecstasy," she confided. "I wait all week for this hour."

Jean explained to her that while an emotional and sexual balance is important in the life of every human being, during a group meeting it is about something else, which requires one's full attention. She changed groups and remarried two years later. His charm worked beyond the norm.

After my first three-month stay in India, I shared my impressions first with Arnaud Desjardins and then with Jean Vaysse. One night when I spoke with him, we disagreed strongly about the implications of the experiences I reported, but by dawn we found that our friendship remained intact. He gave me a copy of a book he had just written, which now exists in German, inscribed with a dedication. I criticized it severely but that did not spoil our friendship either.

His activities continued to increase, consuming more and more of his time and energy. Would he be able to sustain these tireless efforts? I asked myself. This constant over-exertion turned into overwork.

Finally, the answer to my question came — in the negative. In May of 1975, Jean's health suddenly declined. It was lung cancer, already extensive even though he had never smoked. In June, he operated on my aunt again for stomach cancer. She is still alive, healed and well at eighty-six years old. But it was his last operation. He died the following September.

RENÉ ZUBER

My dear Richard, you knew the film director René Zuber. He was in charge of publishing the teachings of Mr. G. and for a certain time provided technical direction for films about the Movements. He was a kind of Don Quixote, tall and emaciated, who took up the smallest causes with the courage of a knight. One couldn't help loving this man whom we nicknamed "the eternally young man." Something emanated from him and went straight to your heart, although his expressions, his way of speaking by slowly stretching his sentences into arabesques and his way of treating every detail seriously as if it were essential, inevitably made you smile.

Zuber was certainly one of the most impractical men I have ever met. Do you remember, Richard, the story of the still unbound books which were stored in Vienna for a long time and which we had to transport to Munich with such endless effort? The bookbinder Scheibe in Vienna had started his work by making the covers red, but René — even though he was not stubborn — made the color of the cover a matter of state. Everything had to be redone in green. Yet we couldn't blame him. He had good and totally honest intentions and his calm manner was disarming.

René Zuber and Claude Renoir, the filmmaker and grandson of the painter Auguste Renoir, were ensigns in the Navy when in July 1940, British battleships appeared in the harbor of Mers-el-Kébir in Oran. Both men were there serving on the battleship Provence. The English gave an ultimatum to the French ships and pointed their cannons at the French fleet. Claude Renoir recounted how René Zuber stood at attention in front of the admiral and said solemnly: "I refuse to shoot the English!"

In spite of this public refusal he was saved from immediate execution, without a council of war, but by the annihilation at that very moment of the French fleet by the British. This massacre left one thousand and six hundred dead, after which Zuber's chivalrous gesture was forgotten.

Zuber lived very close to me in Meudon and we met often. He met Mr. G. in 1942 after having undergone a long psychoanalysis before the war with Doctor René Laforgue, a direct pupil of Sigmund Freud and the first practitioner of psychoanalysis in France.

"Laforgue freed me from my pathologies. Mr. G. helped me find the path to higher development," Zuber told me.

There is no better way to distinguish between psychopathology and psychology. Unfortunately, confusion exists between these two very different domains. What is said about "upward development" is often nothing but a sad jumble.

René was a grateful and devoted student of Mr. G. and

greatly admired his "work" companion Pierre Aboulker. When René fell sick and died at seventy-three years old, he looked only fifty.

OTHERS

You see, my dear Richard, these are some of the traveling companions who left their mark on me. There were many others, less close. The "work" does not have the aim of cultivating friendship, and we rarely saw each other outside of group meetings and certain celebrations.

One of these companions was Gabrielle Franck. Gabrielle came from a wealthy family and became an art dealer during the war mainly to earn money for Mr. G. By then she was quite old, subtle and sensitive, the eldest of three sisters who all were familiar with the evenings at Mr. G.'s apartment. Gabrielle often invited me to her large apartment when I made my weekly trip from Chinon to Paris.

"Before I met Mr. G.," she said, "I was quite spoiled by life. So this effort to make money from artwork has turned out to be useful for me. I didn't need the money, but I was happy to be able to help him this way."

And when I wondered if others had helped him financially during the war, she replied: "Yes of course, but in reality we did it for ourselves. He himself managed very skillfully. He spread the rumor among bankers, shopkeepers, etc. that he owned numerous oil wells in the United States from which the war had separated him and convinced them to give him enormous amounts of credit, debts which his American students actually paid after the war. This was his oil, his students!"

For years, Henri T. led the group to which I belonged, along with Mme. de S. He is still living, very old, but has not reduced his activities as a guide for hundreds of others. I speak of him here because his effective way of teaching the "work" was so valuable to me. I hold him in high esteem but I have no right to comment further. I was his doctor for years. All the more reason to keep quiet.

Michel de S., the son of Mme. de S. was not strictly speaking a friend, though I appreciated him very much for his fine discretion and benevolent intelligence. We had the same profession, which was the basis for our warm yet ironic greetings full of innuendo like "My dear colleague, how are you?" The practice of psychiatry offers a real human experience, and it is acquired with difficulty and gradually, but it is presumptuous to take the theory of psychopathology too seriously.

I would not, my dear Richard, suggest that harmony and calm always prevailed among the people who were following the Gurdjieff teaching. However, our groups generated and expressed less negativity than other professional or social associations in which I have participated. The feeling of honest men and women meeting together has never left me. There were disagreements but never anything, I can attest, dishonorable or petty.

Chapter XII
1948 – PARIS OR CHINON?

At the beginning of 1948, Mr. G. and Mme. de S. announced their plan to travel to New York. Everyone was informed that during their three-week absence, copies of the chapters in the first book of *Beelzebub's Tales to his Grandson* would be available at Mme. de S.' apartment for those who wished to read them from 10:00 a.m. to 12:30 p.m. and from 3:00 p.m. to 5:30 p.m. every day. Mr. G. had set a reading tax payable in francs and different for each copy. Hearing a few chapters read aloud had captivated me, so I rushed to put my name on a waiting list, convinced that there would be a crowd. But there was no list.

It was winter, time to sell my apple harvest. Hence I decided to bring my family to the capital and move in with my in-laws. With the addition of five of us, we were seven, and our living quarters were a bit cramped; moreover, my wife was expecting her fourth child. Even so, her parents were delighted with the decision.

On the first day I arrived at Mme. de S.' apartment before 10:00 a.m. to avoid waiting in a long queue. However, to my great surprise, no one else joined me. I read alone all morning. In the afternoon I was alone again and so the week passed without my being in the least disturbed in my reading. I asked Marthe, who was on duty at the apartment, why no one else had come.

"It seems that everyone is too busy," she replied.

The second week a man came twice, for half an hour each time, more to see Marthe than to read. She therefore decided to cease standing watch and authorized me to take the manuscript home for myself on the condition that I would return it upon Mr. G's return.

I went back to Chinon with my family — earlier than expected — having accidentally left a few chapters of the precious manuscript at my mother-in-law's. The thought of this woman trying for days and days to understand something from this difficult prose made me smile for a long time. She never spoke to me about it, never admitted having attempted to read it, but she sought explanations in a roundabout way from her daughter.

Later when Mr. G. and Mme. de S. returned from America, I brought the manuscript back to Paris and visited Mme. de S. to pay the reading tax. She laughed: "Mr. Gurdjieff only wanted to encourage people to read! We don't appreciate what's free, do we? But you see, except for you, it was of no use. Buy your children something instead!"

When the time came for Mr. G.'s return, I waited with many others on a platform at the Gare Saint Lazare for the Atlantic train from Cherbourg. Mr. G. appeared at the carriage door wearing a black hat, his eyes beaming, laughing. At the sight of him Mme. H. was moved to tears. We surrounded him in a large circle which he glanced over with his calm gaze before declaring: "Still only eating, not working much!"

Then he grabbed the arm of young Robert Godet, who took him home. Godet knew how to use the license granted to fools and shared a rapport with Mr. G. that was more like a connection between comrades than a relationship between master and student.

Several Americans and Englishmen arrived from the New World with Mr. G. I remember Ouspensky's two nieces, one of whom — Tatania a tall blonde and pretty young girl who was a passionate horsewoman in the U.S. — later married Tom Forman, whom you know, Richard. The wife and the daughter of the architect Frank Lloyd Wright got off the train as well, still seasick from the voyage, along with Lonya, Mme. Ouspensky's son, who was walking with Mr. Bennett, Captain Bennett. Lonya was a man of a certain age, very tall and vigorous, who sported an English mustache in a young man's face and was constantly smiling. Later that day he and I dragged in two of the six giant trunks to Mr. G., who told us he had no idea what they contained.

Late that evening, at the feast at Mr. G.'s, Mr. Bennett assumed the role of table manager. He spoke the best English with an Oxford accent, emphasizing the slowness and slight stutter it requires. This accent prevents the rudeness of the most inveterate boor, envelops him and forces him to keep calm. This is how Bennett never lost his composure and provoked smiles, even laughter, from all of the Americans. For the French and the Russians, the assembled company constituted an Anglo-Saxon menagerie.

Strange trio, this Bennett group: Mr. Bennett, his wife Mrs. Bennett, who was about fifteen years older than he, and young Elizabeth, his future wife. Mrs. Bennett, an old and dignified lady, treated Elizabeth with kindness and eagerness. She told me a few days later, in a café on Avenue Carnot: "I was born in India and grew up among elephants and camels. Here in our towns of stone and concrete, where human relationships are equally made of concrete, I always feel like a stranger. In spirit I still live in India."

She spoke French perfectly just like her husband, to whom she gave a nickname that inevitably sparked laughter. She was charming and a great maturity emanated from her: "He and I have a full life behind us," she said to me one day, "with countless adventures. But he is still young and now needs a new young wife. Isn't Elizabeth a wonderful woman for him?"

In fact, everyone noticed it. She added: "I will soon join my ancestors. It is not good for him to stay alone."

She died about fifteen months later. My friend Bernard C. described her as a marvelous being, such as from tales of India. The ease, simplicity and nobility of her manners, the way in which this wise woman stood before Mr. G. and how he treated her, generated only admiration.

In the meantime, my friend Ludolf was getting worse and worse. He suffered from intense pain day and night, and the good Jacqueline could hardly move away from his bed. I would sometimes take a brief walk with her in the nearby Bois de Boulogne. She complained of the impossible living conditions in Ludolf's house where among other misfortunes money was painfully lacking. I could do nothing except help him financially, and the situation oppressed me more and more.

The thought of death, of the irremediable absence of my best friend, was unbearable and I could no longer sleep. On the other hand, and quite naively, the thought of Mr. G.'s immortality came often to my mind. I imagined that he would not suffer bodily death, and in my infantile and admiring incomprehension I saw him as a supernatural being. He delivered me from this illusion, yet something of it stubbornly remained in me.

My anxiety about Ludolf became so unbearable that no longer knowing where to turn, I decided to speak directly to Mr. G. I wanted to ask him to see Ludolf, who lived two minutes from his home, and help him. Full of excitement, I stationed myself in front of his bedroom door after the evening meal. I was sure I would meet him but I also knew how unusual and cavalier, almost indecent, it was to try to intercept him there.

At last, Mr. G. appeared and I asked him for a few minutes of conversation. He looked at me in his calm, thoughtful manner. Then he gestured and led me into a small space called the candy library.

After a moment of silence, I explained to him the tragic situation of my beloved friend, whom he had already seen at his place, and implored him to visit Ludolf to help him. Dramatically distressed, I waited a long time under his calm and compassionate gaze for him to respond. Finally, he said: "I cannot help your friend. I cannot go see him. But you can!"

Then he gave me a sharp look and added: "You, now always come to my apartment whenever you want. No need to ask Mme. de S. anymore. You might be able to help."

I calmed down immediately. My grief remained but the dramatic anguish was alleviated — not so much by Mr. G.'s words, which did not offer the solution I expected — but by his radiant presence. Recognizing his absolute authority, I accepted his answer. I informed Mme. de S. of the new privilege which he had granted me. She recommended caution given the significant number of Anglo-Saxons who were with us.

Medical authorities were consulted for Ludolf and they decided to perform a double operation: one directly against the cancer of the sigmoid, and the other a cordotomy to reduce the pain. A cordotomy is the interruption of the ascending nerves in the spinal cord in order to numb the pain. Ludolf groaned for two weeks after these operations which were done at La Salpêtrière Hospital.

However, he recovered, suffered much less and little by little began to get up and take a few short walks. He now limped, and his right foot no longer responded to his will and hung inert. Yet his condition improved so much that he was able to spend two weeks with us at the Château de Vaugaudry during the summer.

You, Richard, are probably asking me: What exactly was happening in Chinon during this time? You, a journalist who wonders about these things and insists on knowing: "Franz, don't you say anything about your family?"

There is not much to say. In the spring of 1948, there were four children. Two boys — the first Jean-Pierre, already grown up, and the second Sylvain, just born — with two daughters — Marie-Claude and Francine in between. They were all born at home in their mother's bed, in the presence of a midwife, their grandmother and myself, their father. We did not call the doctor. Not that we were suspicious of doctors but it did not occur to us. The midwife, a pretty and vigorous daughter of a merchant from Chinon, came by bicycle approximately every two months to monitor the pregnancies and have lunch with us at the castle. From what I know today, she was very competent in obstetrics, more than most general practitioners. At that time before seeing many possible complications in the hospital, a birth seemed to me the simplest thing in the world.

Their mother breastfed all four children, the first for seventeen months. Never I insist, never, were we woken up at night by a child. I do not believe I ever heard them cry. Never I insist, never, did we consult the doctor for an illness. He came only for a few accidents, the mirror incident I described and two or three times when one of the boys fell while climbing a tree. When Jean-Pierre was eleven years old, we consulted Doctor Benoît on his behalf who enlightened us and remedied his problems without medication. Doctor Benoît, to whom Jean Vaysse had introduced me, was a talented pediatrician and psychoanalyst and remained a family friend.

I would like to point out, my dear Richard, that during all these years we had no health-care coverage. It was only when I was fifty-four that I had to join the welfare system, since it became compulsory for doctors. By then I was already a grandfather with three married children.

My fellow medical students sometimes envied me: One commented, "You are really lucky to be able to learn pediatrics at home!"

But these little darlings taught me nothing, nothing at all. We applied the same measure for everything, colds, tonsillitis, measles and other childhood illnesses: in bed for a few days. As you know very well, Richard, a little flu treated by a doctor lasts about eight days, but only five when it is not treated. This is in no way a matter of boasting. The children grew up in the constant presence of their mother, attentive to the slightest discomfort, as well as Doctor Salmanoff's natural methods such as baths, herbal teas and chest wraps, which helped a great deal.

The questions came later. The proverb: "Little children, little worries, big children, big worries," so widespread in Vienna, was quite relevant. I spent sleepless nights wondering how we ought to educate teenagers. I still do not know, but I have remained faithful to a principle of wisdom anchored in me:

> If you know, act. If you don't know, don't act or say anything. Whatever happens, when in doubt, refrain...

The following years considerably enriched my psychiatric experience. I noticed many times that the usual conversation and chatter on psychological subjects nourished by gossip gleaned anywhere and anyhow cause more damage than anything else.

There is not much to say about my first marriage, nor do I feel that I have the right to talk about it. The decision to leave my family when our youngest son was twenty-one was already developing within me. When the call from India took me away in 1969, Sylvain was actually twenty-one-and-a-half years old. I was greatly surprised to read in a text from ancient India: "A father of a family can leave his wife and children when the last is twenty-one years old." This is surprising, is it not? I did not know that this practice was codified in the precepts of the Indian people and intended for the attainment of inner happiness. I left France with the intention of never coming back. But as you know, things turned out differently.

Life is made up of small events, as the saying goes. Reflecting back on this era at the Vaugaudry estate, it was filled and colored with many episodes and events. I shall tell you about a few of them.

Jean-Pierre at six years old crossed a forest every day to school in La-Roche-Clermault. This is the famous place where Rabelais set the battle of Picrochole during which, among other events, an extraordinary competition took place among certain monks of gluttony and drinking the juice of the vine. The small village was on a hillside composed of low white stone houses and surrounded by vineyards that the inhabitants tended as if they were sanctuaries. The school and the town hall shared a single building as is customary in the villages, facing a narrow street only two meters wide. On the other side there was a charming building, proud of its novelty: that absolute necessity, a public urinal.

Every year in August the town held an auction to sell plots of rushes that it owned. These fields of rushes were divided into plots that were more or less easy to mow and yielded good fodder for the cattle. Otherwise, there was not enough hay for the animals because land was prioritized for the essential crops of vines and fruits. Since I needed some rushes for our horse, I went to the auction.

The same ritual had taken place there for ages. Each farmer brought his strongest wine so that the competitors, tipsy from the "rounds" he offered, were unable to shout fast enough to get a good plot. The quantities of good wine consumed in that single afternoon justified the existence of the charming little building across the street. Though I did not drink much out of simple politeness, I knew little about the value of the plots of rushes and ended up with the worst ones. As a result, our reaping machine broke more than once.

At that time Cinais and Lerné (the birthplace of François Rabelais) were far from any means of public transportation and not even reachable by asphalt roads. The places Rabelais mentions in his books abounded with healers and other miracle workers, all of whom were peasants. Out of pure ethnological interest I visited two of these people, simply to note their robust health and solid capacity to ingest the good nectar of the Chinonais.

The whole region was full of witchcraft, apparitions of revenants, ghosts, and so on. Richard, you the historian, have you heard of Urbain Grandier, who was burned at the stake in the time of Richelieu because the Ursuline nuns of Loudun declared themselves bewitched by him? It is more likely that this young and handsome confessor, a bit of a libertine, turned the heads of the mother prioress and the nuns, who manifested their passion in hysterical dances and thereby alarmed all of France.

Years later a woman by the name of Marie Besnard who lived there from 1950 to 1955 was accused of poisoning twelve men. I knew the man, Mr. Auguste, who started the whole affair. A strange fellow, he had come to see me several times in Vaugaudry about his orchard projects, and I had visited him in Loudun where the notorious criminal trial took place. I looked over his land and visited him in his wizard's lookout, the Montpensier tower. Later a fire completely destroyed it.

I was still living in Chinon when Auguste publicly held Marie Besnard responsible for witchcraft for which the poor woman was accused a year later. Twelve corpses were dug up, soaked in arsenic. This innocent old lady remained in prison for seven years before being acquitted at her third trial thanks to an intelligent defender who proved that the wood of the coffins and the earth of the cemetery contained as much arsenic as the corpses.

I stop. Vaugaudry is part of Touraine, land of secrets in the heart of France, full of a strange and mysterious history. Here can be found the towns of Richelieu and Descartes which are it seems to me the only cities in Europe that have borne the names of two great figures of politics and philosophy for over two hundred years. I am not including Russia, obviously.

Less grandiose are the provincial stories within the walls of Vaugaudry itself. An example is the story of Rosine, a pretty and kind young girl who took care of our children. She could neither read nor write, but she knew many songs and proverbs and loved the little ones in a touching way. They were charmed and returned her affection. She came from a family of ten or twelve children in Cinais, a mysterious village hidden in caves, filled with prehistoric houses that were clean and welcoming, cool in summer and warm in winter.

Rosine sang and played all day with the children and for her own amusement. Working at my desk I couldn't help listening with pleasure. In the kitchen she also served Roger, our faithful and silent servant, a devoted factotum who would never have agreed, as she did, to take his meals with the boss's family. In love with Rosine body and soul, he enjoyed her presence but his extreme shyness kept him from expressing his feelings. She made no response to his silent adoration.

One autumn I hired around fifteen young people from the surrounding area to harvest apples. One of them, a tall and strong fellow with abundant black hair, obviously turned Rosine's heart. This was to the great chagrin of Roger, who henceforth swallowed his soup with gloom and was sometimes heard confiding his sorrow to Brillant, my large draft horse. One day, trusting my friendship, he plucked up his courage and asked me to get rid of the tall, dark-haired fellow who was so bad at picking apples. I said I could do so only after the harvest, which disappointed him. It was too late. Rosine's belly was growing. She buried herself for a while deep in the caves of Cinais and came back to us happy as a finch, her newborn little girl left in the good care of her mother with other little ones. The progenitor had disappeared, certainly busy with other prospects. Yet Roger the taciturn was also tenacious. He married Rosine, and they probably still live today surrounded by a large family. All is well that ends well!

Such was not the case for my neighbor M. Moreau, the mayor of La-Roche-Clermault, who often came to talk with me or make a phone call. Before ten o'clock, when the red nectar of Rabelais, the famous *Breton,* produced its effect, M. Moreau behaved like a very pleasant man. His son Gilbert, just seventeen years old, had seduced a peasant's daughter, and Mme. Moreau quickly arranged a marriage of necessity. Necessity or not, local tradition commanded that the wedding last three days. There was eating, drinking and sleeping in barns.

The young husband nevertheless continued to mingle with the gang of boys who went to the Saturday evening dances by tractor and trailer — private cars being rare in these post-war times. One night as the agricultural carriage bounced across the fields, Gilbert, perched on the hitch, fell off and the loaded trailer crushed him. This young father not yet eighteen years old died immediately. As a local squire, I was offered the place of honor at the funeral feast, the same place I had sat in less than a year earlier at the wedding party. Each time for a few moments I laughed and cried with them.

This was life in Chinon. Meanwhile a host of occupations kept me in the orchards or at the office in town or in the fields from morning to evening, Sunday to Thursday, week after week. I left Vaugaudry to go to Paris on Thursday afternoons, remaining there until late Saturday night. I thus lived in two worlds as I believe I have shown you. Certainly we drank different juices on each of these two planets but we drank both of them equally well!

However, there were significant points where these worlds met. Many similarities and behavioral traits bring Georges Ivanovitch Gurdjieff into comparison with François Rabelais, who lived from 1494 to 1553. Like Rabelais, G. I. G. studied medicine and theology. The most famous of Rabelais' works, *Gargantua* and *Pantagruel,* are analogous in intention and structure to the *Beelzebub's Tales to His Grandson.* The two authors pursue the same goal by the same means: an impartial critique of the life of humanity with the aim of educating the reader. Both take as their hero a being from another dimension, superior to ours. Let the proponents of metempsychosis find material here for exploration! If you find the time, my dear Richard, do not deprive yourself of the pleasure of reading *Beelzebub* as well as *Pantagruel* and *Gargantua.* They are full of life, and the latter marked with the motto "always drink, never die" which is still engraved on all the wine glasses sold in Chinon.

Mr. G. had a tremendous sense of humor and was fond of jokes and pranks, though Rabelais' mischievous tricks are even more famous. In one story Rabelais, in Lyon and penniless, was able to meet King François 1er in Paris. How? His fertile imagination led him to the constabulary where he accused himself of preparing a regicide attack. He was chained and quickly transported to Paris. The king recognized him and rewarded him for his cunning, making the whole court laugh.

Because laughing is healthy and releases unnecessary tension, Rabelais delivered his craft in colorful prose and peppered it with the most unbridled comedy. For example, in the final round of the fart competition, in front of a crowd of connoisseurs, where the winning monk extinguished a lit candle three cubits away with great noise ... And in a similar way how many times did Mr. G. turn around toward Mme. de S.: "Here madame, no *bon ton!*"

He knew that she flinched at every vulgar word and perhaps he thought her all the better for it? He was also preparing for the future.

As for laughter, and outright laughter too, opportunities abounded, especially at lunch at Mr. G's apartment. People with the stiffest seriousness looking like deadpan sphinxes could only come out of their rigidity when Mr. G. started to joke. They laughed and writhed while Mr. G., after triggering thunderous laughter, would observe impassively with an inscrutable expression on his face. It was always the same jokes, yet we always laughed. When we noted our surprise that these hackneyed stories continued to provoke the same outbursts, Mr. G. would reply: "If a good story, good forever."

Mr. Bennett, in his role as table manager with his slightly mannered Oxford accent, his well-bred politeness and constantly provocative questions, proved a source of both playfulness and reflection.

Mr. G. often elucidated his system of human functions in three short sentences, "Body is dirty," "Feelings are stingy," and "Head is stupid," which he illustrated with stories, always in English. He said: "The body is dirty. Body is dirty, that is Irish. This concerns the Irish. An Irish peasant one day left for a distant city with his grandson. To reach it they had to ford a river and so sat down to remove their galoshes and socks. The little one was surprised at his grandfather's feet. 'But grandfather, your feet are completely black!'

"'Do not forget that I am fifty years older than you,' replied the old man."

And then: "The head is stupid. Head is stupid, that is English, Mister Bennett. Three English gentlemen decided together to take a walk. They walked in silence. After an hour, the first one said, 'Nice weather today.'

"Two hours later, the second replied, 'Yes, nice.'

"Then the third, two more hours later. 'I don't want to walk around with such chatterboxes anymore.'"

I no longer remember the story that accompanied "feelings are stingy." Mr. G. probably told it more rarely, but he certainly said: "Feelings are stingy, that is Scottish."

The Scots were often the butt of his jokes that touched on avarice: "In Scotland, you write on the front door of your home: Please wipe your feet on our neighbor's doormat."

I found it remarkable for me one evening when Captain Bennett addressed Mr. G.: "Mr. Gurdjieff — you compare the body, dirty, to the Irish; the head, stupid, to the English; and the feelings, miserly, to the Scots. But to which people, sir, would you compare consciousness?"

Mr. G. slowly turned his eyes on all those present who were expecting a joking response. But the answer came penetrating: "Consciousness is Jewish."

No comment. In the grave silence that followed, everyone pondered and kept to themselves.

Mr. G. went quite regularly to the Russian Orthodox cathedral on rue Daru to attend religious services. I sometimes took him in the car, especially at Easter and Christmas. Opposite the church, there was a store with all kinds of pastries, sweets and Russian products. Sometimes we filled half the car with them.

And so, from the spring of 1948 to the fall of 1949, I took part in the lunch and evening meals at Mr. G's house three or four times a week.

After the harvest we loaded large truckloads with apples that were carefully packed in crates ready for sale. I would leave Vaugaudry around four o'clock in the afternoon by car and take the road to Orléans or Chartres, whose magnificent cathedral superbly displayed its towers lit by the evening sun, an extraordinary vision of Christianity. I would arrive in Paris in the evening and rush to Ludolf's house. Around nine o'clock, I went to Mr. G.'s house, where I stayed until late at night, often one o'clock in the morning. Then I went to Les Halles market where the apple truck was waiting for me.

Then my work began. I assessed the market situation, the prices, and sold quantities of crates to one or another of the wholesalers or to an agent. My presence in person at night at Les Halles meant that my earnings were more than a third higher than those of most fruit growers. After the meal at Mr. G.'s, Les Halles of Paris was a wonderful contrast. Popular and authentic, it was like the belly of the capital, a place of surprising and picturesque scenes of an exclusively nocturnal life.

By the fall of 1948, drawn by an unquenchable desire to practice medicine, I inquired at the university office and discovered that the admission conditions, modified after 1946, now permitted a naturalized war veteran as I was to fulfill the French nationality requirement. The obligatory French baccalaureate had been replaced with a general culture and history exam for combatant holders of a foreign baccalaureate. In addition, special and easier sessions for examinations and competitive examinations were offered to all those who had taken part in the war. I thought about it again and again, weighed the pros and cons and ended up consulting Dr. Conge, a kind and serious doctor whom I had noticed at Mr. G.'s, where he led some of the groups. I showed him my disabled left hand with its stiff fingers and clumsy thumb, and told him that it was the main cause of my decision a few years earlier not to resume my medical studies.

"You certainly cannot become a surgeon," he told me, "but as for other medical fields, you are wrong. This disability does not prevent you from studying or practicing medicine. But remember that you have four children, that you are more than thirty and that after such a long interruption your memory is rusty, which will not make it easy. All of this is worth thinking about. That being said, do not consider your hand an obstacle. Be assured that it is not."

The scale began to tilt slowly toward medical school. I asked Mr. G. himself to whom I had never spoken about my dearest wish. He told me: "You, now not suspicious young man anymore. You already a father, a candidate for responsible man. That, medicine, long story."

A few days later, I was working with a young woman setting the table for the evening meal at Mr. G.'s house when he entered. He scolded the young woman, forbidding her from doing this task: "You are not entitled to this job!"

She and he alone knew why. Then he sat down to speak calmly with John, a charming Englishman with whom I had been in touch for many years. Suddenly he turned toward me and shouted: "Selfish!" with an intensity that pierced my insides. I remained there without further comment, conjecturing about the reasons for this exclamation which I can still hear ringing within me. Was it because of my plan to study medicine? Or was selfishness the chief feature in me? Or what else?

A long interview with Mme. de S. finally helped me make a decision. She encouraged me not to shy away from such a strong desire. But she cautioned that I should not expect miracles from these studies and reminded me that in no case should they make me neglect my inner work. She called her son Michel, already close to the end of his studies, who gave me various useful indications about the faculty of medicine and the Sorbonne.

Then she offered a final conclusion: "Do not be under any illusions. You will not get smarter. These medical studies are pure memorization, a kind of memory training."

"And constant cramming and learning by heart for years," added Michel.

My wife was not against my plan and agreed to return to Paris, although she would miss the beautiful Vaugaudry estate. But it was still necessary to overcome the difficulty presented by my mother-in-law and her pride as a chatelaine-mother.

Chapter XIII
1949 – A CAPITAL YEAR

The year 1949 which I discuss here, my dear Richard, was without doubt a crucial year, one of those turning points when decisive events take place.

At the end of January, I had the opportunity to drive my mother-in-law from Paris to Chinon. I took advantage of the quiet car ride to tell her of my plan to leave Vaugaudry and return to Paris but without mentioning my desire to study medicine. In fact, she showed more disappointment than surprise, and to my relief, my apprehension about her extreme reluctance turned out to be incorrect. Over several days, she reacted in a much more positive way and discussions took place between my wife, her and me, in a constructive manner.

Once my mother-in-law had accepted the fact of our move, we began to attend to the details. She made a proposal that I agreed to in which my wife and I were allocated half of the sum resulting from the sale of the property, less whatever had been paid for the purchase and the expenses of installation, equipment and improvement. Unfortunately, I did not receive this money when the time came. But the heavens proved eager to help and compensated me with the apple crop. The exceptionally abundant harvest of the fall of 1949 ensured the support of my family during my years of study, giving us genuine financial independence.

We faced greater difficulties finding a buyer for Vaugaudry. The search dragged on for an entire year. A man of a certain age, very wealthy and with some knowledge of fruit-growing, was enthusiastic about the property. The deal was almost concluded when he added a condition that made me turn pale. He would have bought and paid for all the property and machinery on the spot and retained the staff if Mr. François Grunwald would stay a few more years to manage the company, decide on new planting and organize the sale of the fruit. This solution was the preference of my in-laws, who were already thinking about other financial investments, but of course I ruled it out. Thank God, my wife and I were part owners of Vaugaudry and nothing could be done without our consent.

This man's request did not flatter me though I was proud of it, and I understood why we absolutely had to sell the property. Keeping it, leaving it in the hands of a manager and overseeing it from afar would have led only to disaster. The attitude of another potential buyer, an agricultural engineer, also fed my pride. Married to a rich heiress, he declared this property too large for his still-limited experience but was so impressed that he returned to visit three times.

During this period of preparation for a new situation, other worries consumed me: in particular my inability to learn. Reviewing the courses I had taken in Vienna, immersing myself in physics, chemistry and biology in view of the medical pre-exams, I became aware that my rusty brain, as Dr. Conge had put it, responded poorly. I was alarmed to see that while the energy spent concentrating and studying for an hour required a superhuman effort, it did not result in my memorizing anything at all.

For eleven or twelve years I had not studied systematically. Re-training myself in how to learn was a bitter and arduous task. I realized that similar to a long jump in athletics, a lengthy run-up would be necessary. This handicap was a fact and after four years of inner work I accepted it as an obstacle I had to overcome.

Meanwhile during February and March of that same year, Ludolf's condition worsened. Barely able to get up and walking with infinite difficulty, he rarely went out. Once, as I walked with him and Jacqueline in the Bois de Boulogne, we nearly had to carry him, and his grateful smile broke our hearts. Already so thin, he was visibly losing weight.

Jacqueline sacrificed herself for Ludolf, and her incessant

efforts were not only accepted but were almost a necessity. Roger, a young and vigorous masseur with a generous heart, worked diligently and sensitively to help her take care of him. He loved Ludolf very much and grew to be my friend. Later he became my favorite teammate when canoeing down rivers.

Mme. Chipiloff the hardworking grandmother was glad to work with Roger, who was a dedicated masseur and a true model of strength and health, compared to Ludolf, a talented but sick dancer. I was sometimes on the receiving end of her complaints, however: "He eats too much. Better eaters are not better workers."

Nice aphorism of masseur wisdom, isn't it?

The good Roger did the impossible in this house where there was constant excitement, while Ludolf was losing weight and suffering nearly continuously.

We formed a strange quintet — Ludolf, Jacqueline, Roger and me — and in contrast, Nadia, Ludolf's wife, agitated but effective. Our love for Ludolf closely linked Jacqueline and me, a bond which we felt consciously and that later persisted...

"Come," she said to me. "When you are here Ludolf is calmer, and that is so appreciated."

In the spring I took Michael, Ludolf's son, to our house in Vaugaudry. A strong friendship immediately formed between him and my son Jean-Pierre. It was a joy to watch these two boys, little devils of six or seven years old playing in the fields, forests and buildings. Freed from the hectic atmosphere of a sick man's home in Paris, Michael blossomed quickly, becoming a cheerful boy with the naturally graceful movements inherited from his father. Even the farm workers, who were usually so unresponsive, admired his spontaneous joy as he danced around a campfire, having fun with the little girls.

Our predecessors at Vaugaudry had left us with their dog, a long-haired Brussels Griffon, as they were unable to accustom him to a new place. Dear old Dax died after a brief illness and we decided to bury him in the forest behind the castle. The two boys sang at the almost solemn ceremony and even cried a little. They had never been able to pronounce Dax, saying Dasq instead.

Dax was a strange dog, in fact. He would remain lying down in front of the dining room in all weather — except when there was a storm, when he would hide in a corner. He was good-natured, letting the children play with him and sometimes even torture him. But woe to the stranger who entered the castle without knowing his name! Dax resisted all attempts of the butcher's boy to charm him when he delivered the meat twice a week. Always angry with the poor delivery man, he bit him several times.

The female dogs left him disinterested and growling, but when a male passed by, large or small, he rushed to attempt to mate with him. So animals too? I was surprised but was told with certainty that this behavior was not rare among dogs.

At the end of 1948 Mr. G. had been given the manuscript of *In Search of the Miraculous: Fragments of an Unknown Teaching* by the talented writer P. D. Ouspensky, based on his notes on the work of the Moscow group between 1915 and 1921. Ouspensky had died in London the previous year after returning from a trip to New York. Most of his students joined Mr. G. in Paris. Others created groups of their own which sooner or later were lost in the sands. Mr. Bennett had been in constant contact with both Mr. G. and Ouspensky, separating from them only during the war, when he held the post of Under-Secretary of State for Coal in the Churchill government.

Ouspensky had stated in his will that publication of his manuscript was subject to the personal approval of Mr. G., who had not read any book for a long time. Mme. de S. was ready to study the manuscript when Mr. G. unexpectedly took hold of it and immersed himself in this English text for several days. We waited in suspense for his comments.

He was positive: "Piotr Demianovitch, good journalist, really good journalist. Everything in there is true, are facts. We can get it published, Madame, and also translated to French and to German."

Mme. de S. quickly undertook the translation, working with Henri Tracol and Philippe Lavastine, who was finally able to arrange publication in Paris by Stock under the title: *Fragments of an Unknown Teaching* at the same time as the English original was being published in London and New York.

It is impossible to describe the eagerness with which we threw ourselves into this book, spending nights reading and rereading it! Everyone wanted to talk about it in their groups, but we wisely agreed that we had to digest it before commenting or asking questions. The publication had caused a stir in Paris and France. Certain newspapers made their comments of course, illustrated with photos from the Fontainebleau era mixed with gossip about Katherine Mansfield.

Over time this faithful report from the first Moscow group changed the atmosphere and the "work" of our groups. Two or three years later and before the publication of *Beelzebub* and of *Meetings with Remarkable Men*, this text became so popular that it served as an obligatory reference book. It satisfied the curiosity of those who, like me, had joined after the war and surrounded the few members of Mr. G.'s wartime Parisian group in an aura of mystery. We could now get an idea of their actual work. Soon, oral readings of certain chapters of Ouspensky's book were organized followed by discussions with questions and answers.

Obviously, this text fascinated me. However, the image I had of Mr. G. from spending time with him did not fit the picture drawn by Ouspensky. Still, like the folds made to a blank sheet of paper that remain visible, even immutable, the book made an enduring impression on me. As I recall, although I was certainly not with him at every moment, far from it, Mr. G. never mentioned the book again.

Mme. de S. suggested that I invite Mr. G. and some of his former students to the Château de Vaugaudry and asked me to help her find a house surrounded by a garden near Paris where he could stay and rest. He was tired, almost sick, she told me, although I had not noticed.

I stood ready one afternoon to extend my invitation, happy to welcome him to our beautiful province. He smiled mischievously: "I cannot come to your house, but you can come with me. The day after tomorrow, big trip to Vichy."

But I could not. For a thousand reasons I had to return to Vaugaudry. I regretted this deeply — not to have taken part in Mr. G.'s last trip in France — especially later, when my friends Bernard C. and John M. told me about their series of adventures, the alternation of fun and seriousness. Mr. G. had invited me so kindly and it seemed to me later that I should have been able to overcome the difficulties that kept me in the countryside.

It was always surprising to witness the direct and trusting contact that Mr. G. knew how to create with simple people. He had a talent for spontaneously establishing a natural and pleasant relationship with anyone. Once during lunch the front doorbell rang. It was the postman bringing a package. Mr. G. invited him in and began a conversation with him about his job, right there in the midst of all the guests gathered around the table. Then the postman, clearly feeling comfortable, said: "What can I tell you, Mr. Gurdjieff? Working is a necessity for me. Not just to make money but it's how I learn about the world."

Mr. G. got up, poured him a glass of Armagnac, filled his own glass, and toasted with him. Then he solemnly declared to everyone around the table: "Exactly like that you must speak. Work is necessary." He then offered the postman a bottle of old cognac, a precious rarity in 1949.

During this last year I went almost every Saturday morning to the steam baths with Mr. G., often giving him a ride. Since I was the only French-speaking person in this assembly of eight or ten Americans and Englishmen, we spoke English. To join the small circle of hammam participants, one had to fulfill a condition that Mr. G. gave to each person the first time: "Obligation to tell a good story, funny and short. Maybe a little saucy but not vulgar. We men, not thugs."

I do not remember what I managed to jabber in my broken English, which was often too clumsy to allow me to understand other people's jokes — except those expressed in Gurdjieffian Russian-English. Mr. G. was especially fond of a Yiddish expression, the untranslatable: "*tzimmes.*" Do you know this word, Richard? *Tzimmes* means that which in a story or a business is essential, extraordinary, original, remarkable, or deserves to be remembered. As soon as someone would get lost in endless speeches, Mr. G. would stop them with a simple: *"Tzimmes?"*

Mr. G. frequented two hammams in Paris: the distinguished and chic one located behind the Opera, and the rather run-down Jewish baths on rue des Rosiers. He preferred the latter because, as he said: "There they understand something about steam, humid, good for the body."

However, we were often in a hurry, so we went to the Opera bathhouse, where the excessively dry heat caused a burning sensation when we breathed. The staff of this elegant bathhouse treated Mr. G. with special consideration, calling him "the General"— perhaps because of his silent and impressive demeanor and his laconic remarks, or perhaps because of his tips.

In the small room we would lie down on wooden slats one above the other to sweat in the intense heat. Mr. G. sometimes gave a detailed inventory of the numerous scars on his arms, legs, stomach, and back: "Those, memories. Here a souvenir from Afghanistan, a stray bullet. It was not intended for me."

He also noticed the scars from my wounds on my arms, thighs and legs: "Where that come from?" he asked.

"From the Italian War, sir."

"Nothing in body and head?"

"No, not even an appendicitis scar, I still have it!"

He continued to examine the bodies of others, pointing at the scars of various wounds. Then he concluded: "Earth, not safe place!"

After this burning heat, Mr. G. quickly immersed himself in a small pool of ice water. I hesitated at first before understanding that the body cools slowly in cold water after experiencing such unbearable heat. Thus, one must dive in quickly before the body turns lukewarm.

Friday was the women's day in the hammam and Mr. G. entrusted a woman with the task of taking those who wanted to go there. "Here in the West," he said, "most human beings have a bad smell because they don't go to the hammam. Only the hot steam and heavy perspiration squeeze the dirt out of the pores. Routine baths and washes are not enough. I can already sense from afar whether someone is going or not going to the hammam."

How he made this distinction when we arrived at his apartment remains a mystery, since the scent of oriental spices filled the staircase and permeated the rooms with a strong, rather pleasant aroma.

Chapter XIV

DEATH OF LUDOLF

By the end of April or the beginning of May, Ludolf's state, already degraded, had worsened. Constantly suffering, he became nothing but skin and bones. Jacqueline remained at his bedside day and night. I went to see him often, staying for a long while each time. My visits did him good but were even better for me because of our meaningful conversations. As much as it seemed to me that his physical strength was diminishing, the strength of his soul was growing and his spirit was rising to levels he had never attained before.

Jacqueline surrounded him with her presence, yet she was constantly subjected to orders from members of the household, which were given without the slightest regard for her or her own health. She was pale and her cheeks were hollow.

"Jacqueline cannot take it anymore," Ludolf said to me one day. "She's exhausted, but without her I feel lost. Please take her to the Bois de Boulogne for an hour or two from time to time."

As we walked under the trees, Jacqueline expressed the loneliness she was already feeling when she thought about the imminent end of our beloved friend.

"He is worried about his children, and he is counting on you," she told me. "I am counting on you too."

She used the word *tu* for "you." We had always said *vous* to each other and this spontaneous informality went straight to my heart.

Another time as we walked through the woods in the rain I saw that her feet were soaked. I examined her shoes and realized that the soles had holes and were torn.

"But why don't you wear decent shoes when it rains?"

"They are my only pair," she replied.

Stunned, I questioned her further. Since I came only for visits, I did not know much about the circumstances of life in the house. I often gave her money for Ludolf but Jacqueline never asked for anything for herself.

I learned that in this hive where she worked all day and watched over Ludolf at night, she didn't receive a single penny. I took her to the first shoe store on Avenue des Ternes, determined to buy her three pairs of shoes and ten pairs of stockings. I explained that the expense was nothing in my budget — indeed, that very morning I had acquired five thousand new crates and spent a fortune on insecticides and fertilizers — but in vain. She accepted only a single pair of shoes to which I insisted on adding slippers and a few stockings. I was extremely upset, but with whom could I discuss the situation? Certainly not with Ludolf. And for all sorts of reasons, not with Nadia. That would have only led to useless discussions.

By the end of May the orchards were keeping me in the countryside, preventing me from coming to Paris for extended visits though I telephoned Ludolf almost every evening. He was weak and his condition remained unchanged.

The trees were now covered with small green apples and promised abundance but only if the necessary treatments were applied at the right times to protect the apples from insects and fungi. This work had to be particularly thorough, the products well-chosen according to the wind and weather, and the trees treated again after the rain. The treatments consumed considerable sums of money and required my presence because, according to many fruit growers, only the one whose wallet is at stake can sense the opportune moments with the necessary diligence.

One afternoon Mme. H. called me on the phone. In a serious tone she told me: "If you want to see your friend still alive, come right away. For the last two days Ludolf has hardly been able to speak but an hour ago he made me understand that I should call you. I too would like you to be here; it would be of great help to me. You know my affection for him. He is an extraordinary man and I'm having a difficult time with what I'm witnessing here. He is completely transformed, I don't know how, and says things to me that are sometimes quite mysterious."

"I'm coming," I replied.

I could not leave until I had attended to some urgent and essential matters. I finally left Chinon at seven o'clock, drove past Tours and followed the Loire River. In Blois as darkness was descending, strange thoughts crossed my mind: "Why does this leave me so cold? The death of my true friend whom I love with all my heart is imminent and I feel nothing, neither warmth nor sadness. Why?"

When I entered his room around ten o'clock in the evening a shiver of fear passed through me, as though something unknown had struck me and left its mark. It was not a dying person lying there; it was death itself, incarnate, personified — an unforgettable encounter. Two people had lifted him with difficulty and held him as he sat on the edge of the bed. He seemed to be in less pain. In his yellowish-white face the high cheekbones were tinged with blue-gray, and his eyes, sunk deeply in their sockets, looked into the distance, fixed and radiant.

Mme. H. seemed to sense my shock at this ghostly encounter and the dismay that filled me. She gave me a sign indicating that she felt the same way, yet this aspect seemed to escape the others who had not left him all day.

Ludolf saw me, greeted me slowly with a weary gesture and with a voice I had never heard before, as if coming from the depths, said to me: "So you came after all. I have been waiting a long time. For years I have been waiting for you."

Then he told the others: Lay me on the bed and leave me with François.

"Are you in pain, Ludolf?" I asked him.

"No, no, I feel nothing anymore," he replied in the same deep tone to which I was gradually becoming accustomed.

Slowly my fear subsided. I stayed near him all night. I began to feel different, in a state I could hardly describe. All my attention turned to Ludolf, who was summoning it with all his might.

Lying calmly on the bed, his head and chest raised by several pillows, he spoke softly to me. He began by expressing how much the inner work of a human being is necessary for others: "What we call consciousness and regard as our own and personal good is in reality only the reflection of a permanent and perpetual consciousness which has never been born and cannot disappear. It is our privilege to participate in this consciousness as human beings. Our understanding consists of this: to submit one's individuality, which everyone falsely presumes that he owns, to this ever-present reality. In general, we imagine that consciousness exists in ourselves. In whom? In you François? In me? In this bodily envelope that I will soon leave? It is a superstition, a fiction, an error. Everything that we designate by 'I' or 'we' — that is to say what is unique to each person — belongs to the great eternal consciousness."

His voice seemed to come from another realm. His expression, his face with its strange smile impressed me more deeply than the content of his words, the full meaning of which I understood only later. Each of his words was imprinted in my memory and remained there.

On the other hand, I no longer remember my own response. I saw only that it caused him a joy that kept growing. Time was disappearing. He continued, not seeming to suffer nor even feeling any pain:

"Wisdom understood as profound knowledge is the true goal of every human life. I was aware of it from the beginning — I mean, from the moment I met Mme. H. and Mr. G.

"I also felt that when I was quite young, I was better prepared than many others thanks to the many painful experiences I had to go through in my life.

"Then I realized that my bodily strength was decreasing and, in recent years as I began to plan for my premature departure, I wanted to pass on this knowledge, born from experience, to you. To you because you are my friend. Unfortunately, for my part I have not always had the necessary strength and for your part, you have not always had the essential availability to receive. Let's make up for these shortcomings at all cost, shall we?

"From now on you must fight this inner battle for both of

us and thus work for the true good of others as well. Of course, I would like to ask you if you want it, if you are ready for this and to wait until you are, but we no longer have the time, and I couldn't bear a refusal or a hesitant answer right now. My dear François, I cannot order you, but I put the task before you.

"Clearly, you absolutely must make your life, for you and for me, of such value that others benefit from it, that it helps them. You must prepare for it by instructing yourself in this path and following this teaching which I have brought you. After this preparation, if you never lose sight of the spiritual happiness of your fellow men, I believe you will be able, if circumstances require it, to go toward other paths. But only after long and conscientious preparation. In my opinion, you should resume your medical studies — not to turn yourself into a walking encyclopedia, obviously — but to acquire in the exercise of this delicate profession more serious in-depth experience."

I listened, totally captivated by his words, overwhelmed. Tears were streaming down my cheeks, of joy and sorrow, both lifted to great heights. I accepted the supreme responsibility that his love was giving me and showed him my assent and total commitment.

Then to my surprise he sat up on his own with great energy — he who had not been able to move without help for a week — and remained upright on the bed. His eyes sparkled. A sublime force radiated from him, much more intense than the physical force of his poor body. He kissed me and I hugged him: "You will be standing for both of us from now on," he said.

He remained thus upright, his gaze luminous, radiant, for a few more minutes. His strength penetrated me as if permeating my trembling body. Against all expectations, this force was filled with happiness and energized by a deep joy. The result was a state that I cannot name: as if I were participating in an elation that did not belong to me. It contained no sadness, no anguish or emotion of that nature. Then he sank slowly onto his pillow.

He spoke to me again in a low voice, his eyes wide open, about his children Michael and Louba; about Jacqueline, who would have to live through difficult times after he was gone; and about Nadia, the mother of his children whose incessant activity he forgave: "She is not guilty for the failure of our marriage," he told me. "We did not understand each other. It's my fault too."

Then his voice weakened until it became inaudible. Around five o'clock in the morning he sighed twice and I felt something move away from him. What to say? His spirit left him, I cannot find another way to say it. For me it was then that he died.

However, his body was still breathing, though slowly. In agony now he no longer spoke. He neither ate nor drank. A single groan sometimes came from his mouth. This state lasted for five days.

I lay down fully dressed on a small couch not far from him and fell asleep. Around seven o'clock Jacqueline woke me up. Then she looked at Ludolf who was moaning softly.

"He has already been like this for several days," she said to me. "Yesterday and last night, he was a little better because of the arrival of Mme. H. and you."

For me, Ludolf was dead. I did not tell anyone. I never told anyone what happened that night. Now forty years later, I am speaking to you about it, Richard. All of this needs to be said.

Then Jacqueline added: "You are pale and unshaven. You look frightening."

A taxi took me to my in-laws' house, near the Gare du Nord. The driver turned to me for a moment: "Are you not okay, sir? Do you want me to take you to a doctor? I know a good one."

When the cleaning lady opened the door of the apartment, my mother-in-law saw me in the hallway and fell unconscious onto the carpet. My father-in-law, who was having breakfast, got up and turned as pale as a sheet when he saw me. Nothing surprised me. I did not say a word. My in-laws knew Ludolf's end was near and believed him to be dead. When I denied it they were surprised, and I too was surprised to deny what seemed obvious to me, that his life had ended.

Mme. de S., whom I telephoned, received me immediately. Seeing me enter and without saying a word, she brought me something to eat and drink. This maternal concern helped me very much, especially since I had not eaten anything since lunch the day before. I spoke to her about Ludolf and my feeling of having seen him leave that night even though he was still breathing. I never said anything about it again. She advised me to rest before coming to Mr. G.'s for lunch.

Slowly, my inner turmoil abated. Bit by bit I became a normal man again. After having bathed, shaved and rested briefly at the Bretonnières' house, I regained a civilized appearance. I returned to see Ludolf before going to Mr. G's apartment on rue des Colonels Renard.

Ludolf was breathing imperceptibly just as when I had left him a few hours earlier, inert in his bed, silently watched over by Jacqueline. Again I knew that his spirit, his soul, as is said, had left the envelope that lay there. I remained near him for a moment, disturbed but quite distant, in front of this body in which I no longer saw him, keeping the memory of the previous night alive and precious.

At Mr. G.'s, Lord Pentland, as tall as he was thin, who would later lead the teaching in the United States, assumed the role of table director in the place of honor. I really liked the calm quality of this level-headed man, who seemed gifted with an inner fire. His six-year-old daughter occupied her place seriously at the table. Mr. G. would sometimes put her next to him and explain how to pour drinks, along with the meaning of the task.

This time the silence before the meal began was longer than usual, impressing me more than ever, as if colored by a serious mystery. With delicate movements Mr. G. mixed the different salads, filled the small bowls and offered them to some of his guests. For the first time he passed one to me, accompanying it with a long look and a few simple words: "You, very hungry man."

I understood his words on a spiritual level. In that respect, truly, I was hungry.

For some time now, after meals Mr. G. would play a small instrument, a kind of portable harmonium that I often saw in southern India, handling the bellows with his left hand and improvising a melody on the keyboard with his right. We recorded this music on one of the first tape recorders which someone had brought from America. These tapes are certainly still available.

He would ask us: "Which do you want? Good liquor or music?"

To which we inevitably responded: "Music." Sometimes however, the thought arose in me that good alcohol would be welcome, thus showing me that I was a bundle of contradictions.

Mr. G.'s musical improvisations were sublime, marvelous, and would bring me to an inner state with a particular taste, a nostalgia for another world that was somehow tinged with melancholy. Since he had been up since five in the morning, he would often doze off after playing his instrument for an hour and we would slip away in silence. It was four o'clock in the afternoon.

Once while we were listening to these melodious improvisations, I saw a woman of a certain age crying, shaken by sobs and overwhelmed with emotion. I recognized her as the author Kathryn Hulme, who wrote the book *Undiscovered Country*, published in 1966. In it she describes at length her meeting with Mr. G. While the German translation, *Unendecktes Land* is decent, the French version — as I have already told you, Richard — seemed to me to be a failure.

I telephoned Chinon several times a day. The orchard manager insisted that my presence was essential, but I decided to wait until the next day before returning. For one thing, I was not able to drive at night and, for another, I did not want to leave suddenly, not wishing to imply an indifference that I did not feel at all. It was simply that Ludolf was no longer there and the unchanging agony moved slowly toward its inevitable end.

At Vaugaudry, although I was caught up in activity, I called the Schild house twice each day. Nothing changed. Ludolf never opened his eyes again. It was Nadia who informed me three days later by telephone of his objective death. He was no longer breathing.

I returned to Paris to stay near and watch over him for two nights as he lay on his deathbed. His male comrades from the groups also took turns visiting his remains every two hours as a sign of esteem and affection. You know some of them, Richard. Henri T. and Albert B. for example, who did not hide their emotions.

I placed his light and icy body in the coffin by myself alone. I did not want others to touch him. Then four of us carried him to the funeral car. A family friend, a Protestant pastor whom I did not know, held a simple and very touching service for the dead in a church close to the Avenue de la Grande Armée. I happened to pass by this church later and each time I did so over the next forty years I would be overcome by the same emotional memory of that moment. I had agreed for the children not to attend the funeral service, though I am less sure now of the correctness of my decision.

Nadia, Mme. H., Jacqueline and I were seated with the coffin in the funeral van as we traveled to the Pantin cemetery. We took the lead in the procession, followed by our friends in their cars. This stiff and anonymous cortège making its way through the heavy traffic suddenly overwhelmed me with revulsion. I became more and more upset as we entered a gigantic cemetery that seemed like a mass grave. My private feelings were so hurt that I immediately expressed them to Mme. H. who urged me to participate in the social ritual until it was over. "Singling yourself out serves no purpose," she whispered in my ear, "other than risking a further disturbance in your intimate feelings."

Today I believe a cremation to be much more dignified.

Mme. H. and I insisted to Nadia that we organize a funeral meal at home that would bring together the members of the group and their local friends as is customary in the French countryside, a custom rich in meaning that symbolizes the continuation of life.

We immediately purchased all kinds of provisions from the neighborhood. Mme. H. presided over the meal, dignified and without sadness. I am absolutely certain that Ludolf, whom we all loved and who brought us together, would have appreciated this celebration in his name. But his Russian mother-in-law, shocked and exasperated, sulked alone in her room, cursing the flighty "Franzuskis" who had been afflicted with such levity.

The next day my sister Hanna arrived from London. I waited for her at the station, happy to see her again, but unable to tell her about the events of the last few days. She was too foreign to understand them and with her I changed worlds again. On the same day I took my sister, Jacqueline, Michael, the adorable four-year-old Louba and a lot of luggage in my big car for a stay in the countryside.

It was the beginning of June. The heat spread in a heavy wave. In the car everyone was asleep except Jacqueline who, sitting behind me, spoke quietly in my ear. I was touched. She was sharing her feelings, full of pain. Who else could she have gone to? I was supporting her tenderly, with Ludolf. I was her lifeline and for my part, I could no longer hide my early love under the guise of friendship. It was that day in the moving car that we exchanged our first kiss. With a full heart I arrived at the castle.

Denise and the children had prepared a festive welcome for us. Ludolf and Nadia's little ones quickly regained their strength. Naturally the love that linked me to Jacqueline, this beautiful young woman, could not remain platonic. However, our relationship, which lasted two years and which we surrounded with the necessary discretion, engendered in Jacqueline a perpetual guilty conscience toward my wife. They esteemed and loved each other sincerely. Denise knew of my affection for Jacqueline and did not take umbrage until the day she discovered in my clothes a long letter from her, which left not the slightest doubt about the nature of our relationship.

That being said, because I loved Jacqueline, I did not want to lock her into a secret affair with no future. Two more years were needed for her to gradually agree to take another course in her life. My medical studies, long and difficult, then began. About four years after Ludolf's death, she married a good and sympathetic man who in time gave her four children. She remained friends with Denise almost more than with me, as my medical studies absorbed my time and energy completely and for a long time.

A film or a novel could have persuasively chosen this extraordinary woman as a main character. In order for the story to be credible however, the novelist would have had to erase a large part of her natural charm. She detested hearing herself praised for her angelic patience, the constant efforts she had made in Ludolf's house and the quality of the attentive service she rendered to him. In this case as in many others, the lived reality is more marvelous than any fiction.

Jacqueline had been participating in Mme. de S.'s most advanced Movements class in the front row. She controlled her movements perfectly with grace. Mme. de S. offered her an opportunity to lead a class of Movements but she refused, declaring in all sincerity, perhaps with a touch of annoyance: "My body has been taught and developed by dance and it understands. But I cannot follow the ideas. I come with you because I loved Ludolf and I respect many other members of the groups. I trust them. But I don't understand with my mind."

She took part in the first two or three Movements films, stayed in the groups for a few years, then moved on elsewhere.

Chapter XV

YOU! — DEUTSCHER OBERLOKOMOTIFCONDUKTOR

My dear Richard, yesterday, Thursday, September 24, 1987, I returned to my sanctuary in the countryside. The volume of cars on the highway caused the usual problems: slowing down, frequent stops, accidents. I even passed burning vehicles. Once I was on the country roads I could finally let my thoughts return to the summer and fall of 1949.

Many people agree that no one really knew Mr. G.: his students and disciples, some of his acquaintances and in particular the Russian emigrants. We can relate events and anecdotes that we experienced with him as I do here, Richard, but the whole of his person remains impossible to grasp. The countless unexpected occurrences left one alternately surprised, amazed, moved or ashamed, delighted or upset or even bursting into laughter.

I am content like many others before me to describe my impressions as simply as possible. Those who have written about Mr. G. saw only their own mirror image reflected back at them. The rascal, scoundrel, philanthropist and saint thus appear as involuntary self-portraits of the writer. Louis Pauwels' book *Monsieur Gurdjieff* provides the best proof of this. The gross untruths it contains describe only their author.

I have often heard that Mr. G. wore a mask in front of others. Sometimes, perhaps. However, I support this assertion from a more unusual and quite tenacious viewpoint: What if he was so disconcerting precisely because he alone showed himself with his face uncovered in front of all of us, in front of all who met him? And what about our identification with our own masks?

This is why, it seems to me, some experienced the unbearable in front of him. And if a deep sadness emanated from his eyes, this expression of regret, didn't everyone see in those eyes only their own image of themselves?

Shortly after my first return from India I spent a day with Arnaud Desjardins. He spoke at length about his Indian master, then asked me to describe Mr. G. to him, whom he had not known but about whom he had heard so many contradictory things. I esteem Arnaud very much and consider him a true friend. Throughout the years I followed the stages of his spiritual development, his total sincerity and honesty, more clearly than the accounts of my other contemporaries. He did not hide anything and spoke openly about his experience and behavior, both the most pleasant and the least honorable. I didn't want to answer him superficially.

My indelible impression, I told him, is that Mr. G. was made of a different stuff than the rest of us, as if he had come from another planet to communicate something that our terrestrial intelligence cannot easily grasp. An immense force emanated from him, until his passing — a force yes, that the people he met received in diverse ways according to their own level. It could become a sexual response, or a purely emotional one, or turn into an irrepressible terror. Some saw in him a luminous angel — others, the devil himself, an accomplished scoundrel or an altruistic saint. I, François Grunwald, constantly felt a goodness, a generous source of inner energy, free from sentimentality. Even his terse remarks and angry outbursts proceeded from kindness and compassion. But I am only one among others and was not the closest to him, far from it.

On the other hand, my dear Richard, the actions of two people who were much closer to him shed very different lights on him, at odds with each other: Roger Godet and Louise Prudhon.

Roger Godet, may his tormented and untimely departed soul rest in peace, a sort of provocative Parisian d'Artagnan, second or third Dan black belt, directed the judo club he had founded where I practiced. Cultivating an audacity and temerity with Mr. G. that bordered on indecency, Godet enjoyed, as I have already said, the freedom of a court jester — up to a point, admittedly. Mr. G. instigated incredible bets with him which Godet inevitably lost. He often told me about them after the fact: "It is still an enigma for me to this day. Why did I always fall into Mr. G.'s trap and almost always in the same way? We didn't bet for fun; the stakes were often considerable. When we started talking about it and negotiating the bet I inevitably had the feeling that I was playing a scam, cheating everyone. I would win; it was obvious. However, Mr. G. always managed to introduce an execution clause that seemed minor and acceptable to me, which then would prove decisive for his victory."

For example, Godet boasted in front of Mr. G. about owning one of the fastest cars in Paris, a recent Bugatti model that could reach two hundred kilometers per hour. Mr. G. drove an old Citroën, fifteen horsepower, known for its heaviness, sturdiness and slowness. He provoked Godet: "I bet two cases of Celtic cigarettes me and my car win a hundred-kilometer race against you."

He smoked these Celtics, which were difficult to obtain on the black market. Godet laughed at him: "You and your old lemon against me and my Bugatti? Best if you give me the two cases of cigarettes straight away. You will save yourself a lot of trouble!" Then, with a disgusted look, he added, "To make a bet where he is absolutely sure to win is not worthy of a gentleman."

Mr. G. insisted on the wager. They discussed and worked out the conditions. The race would take place on a fairly steep road between Lyon and Clermont-Ferrand. Mr. G. demanded that the drive be divided into two sections of approximately fifty kilometers each and that during the first part of the race Godet would be forced to follow him twenty meters behind. The real race would start afterward. The immense advantage that his car possessed led Godet to accept all the conditions.

"I got into my Bugatti," he told me, completely sure to prevail this time. "But in less than two hundred meters I knew I was going to lose again. During the fifty kilometers, Mr. G. drove at around ten miles an hour. His sturdy old motor could handle it, while mine was falling apart. My Bugatti, built for high speeds, heated up considerably. The engine did not completely fail but arrived ruined at the end of the first stage. During the second stage, Mr. G. took unprecedented risks on this road, pushing his C-15 Citroën to the maximum. I was unable to overtake him with my damaged engine. Old devil, he knew mechanics!"

Godet was afraid of being afraid. This was the chief feature which pushed him toward the most impossible adventures, as if relentlessly proving to himself that fear did not affect him. But there are different qualities of fear, and several times when his antics went beyond the acceptable, he was permanently thrown out of the groups by Mr. G. He would then get down on his knees and beg with touching fervor for permission to stay. Mr. G. always gave in, sometimes to the great regret of Mme. de S. and others.

Godet sincerely loved Mr. G. This was his weakness, or perhaps his strength. "I could not help stretching Mr. G.'s patience to the limit," he told me, "always and in all circumstances. But I couldn't have borne a separation from him."

And at Mr. G.'s funeral this daring provocateur wept heartily.

Godet told me about another unforgettable episode. One evening he stayed with Mr. G. until two o'clock in the morning. There had been nearly sixty people at the meal and huge stacks of dishes were piled in the kitchen. The person who usually took care of cleaning-up was absent and not expected until the next morning. Godet had forgotten a briefcase and documents when he left, so he returned to rue des Colonels Renard around eight o'clock the next morning to get them. He couldn't believe his eyes. All the clean dishes were neatly arranged on the shelves in the spotless kitchen. The old man had spent half of his very short night at this solitary work. "I did not say anything," Godet told me, "but I had tears in my eyes all morning." Unlike Mr. G., Godet was a sentimental man.

Godet died around 1960 when the plane he was piloting crashed in India in the foothills of the Himalayas. Freddy L., a friend of mine, was called to the site of the crash because his address had been found with the dead man. This gave him great difficulty with the Indian administration. India prohibited the retrieval of objects that were lying in the wreckage of the destroyed but unburned plane. The gas tank was empty as if Godet had forgotten to fill it before taking off or had mistakenly estimated his course.

With Louise Prudhon on the other hand, I never exchanged a word, but she stands out in my memory as a saint. Small, with gray hair and a round reddish face, she was always dressed in black or dark gray. One could hardly find anyone more subdued than this elderly unmarried nurse.

At dinners she was regularly seated next to Mme. de S. opposite Mr. G., with bright eyes and a transfixed face. He called her "the mother" even though she had never had a husband or children and treated her with an unusual consideration and kindness that he showed no one else. He sometimes spoke to her in a very warm tone which aroused in me, a new person, a natural curiosity about this modest woman.

I ran into Louise Prudhon in other circumstances, not only at Mr. G's apartment. I spent my first two years of medicine at the Hôtel Dieu, a large hospital located on the Île de la Cité, between the Prefecture of Police and Notre-Dame de Paris. It often happened that after my shift I would sit for a moment in the cathedral to collect myself or, if you like, to meditate in the tranquility of this sacred place which was deserted between one and two o'clock in the afternoon. It was the time of day when visitors, busy at lunch, no longer clicked their heels on the flagstones or cackled about the architectural splendors of the house of God in accordance with their usual unworthy behavior. Several times I saw someone kneeling in front of the altar in a recess to the side not far from me, and recognized Louise Prudhon, "the mother" of Mr. G. Immersed fervently in prayer, she was deeply collected, her face transfigured.

I heard about her again when I moved from the medical department to the surgical department. I learned that an extraordinary head nurse was in charge of the ward for the seriously injured and dying. There, I was told she performed real miracles and feats of dedication. Doctors esteemed her to the point of veneration. I was busy elsewhere, however, and rarely saw her, as she was busy too in her nurse's uniform.

At Louise Prudhon's death all the hospital staff gathered around her coffin in the hospital courtyard to pay homage and participate in the especially solemn funeral. Everyone was there, including the heads of departments and the most famous doctors. Professor Besnard, the most renowned and senior doctor at the Hôtel-Dieu, made a speech that began with these words: "Louise the nurse died here at her place of work, where for almost forty years her tireless labor and extraordinary dedication inspired the admiration and esteem of all of us. I have known her and seen her at work for over twenty-five years and I can attest to this."

The huge funeral procession — composed of doctors, nursing staff, perhaps sick people but no relatives — proceeded solemnly to the nearby cathedral where the Archbishop of Paris celebrated a mass for the dead.

For Louise Prudhon it is useless to write of wishing peace for her soul, because this peace, which I perceived only from a distance, was granted to her while she was still on earth.

In August 1949, before beginning the large apple harvest I took Ludolf's children and mine, plus Denise and Jacqueline, by car to Berck-Plage, toward the north of the Manche department. Nadia's mother had established this seaside resort, a rehabilitation institute for the physically disabled, before the war. The resort was greatly damaged during the landing and subsequent liberation battles but had been partially rebuilt in 1949. Mrs. Chipiloff and Nadia were known throughout the region for their work there.

Nadia had also invited Mme. H. to join us so she could take a vacation after a year of work. "Mr. G. came here a few days ago with a Russian emigrant," Mme. H. told us. "He was amused for a while by the hustle and bustle of the crowd on the beach, watching everything with a kind expression and an indulgent smile, and then he left."

Though Berck-Plage tended to be cold and windy, the

weather was beautiful and warm during our stay and the children enjoyed the wonderful beach made of pale, fine sand. Unfortunately, Jacqueline fell ill. Were the surroundings weighing on her? Were they reviving her memories? I worried about her weakness and successive dizzy spells and opened up about it to Mme. H.

Mme. H. was not blind and knew us well, having right away understood our affection for each other. She said to me: "This affair cannot have a satisfactory outcome — either for you, François, or for Jacqueline. It is likely to bring unpleasant complications and in this regard I fear Nadia's reactions more than those of Denise. In the meantime, after everything that has happened, you must continue to support Jacqueline. She has transferred to you what she felt for Ludolf and only time, the greatest of doctors, will be able to heal her."

In September the main harvest began. My orchard manager, Mr. Lavenne, helped me organize everything. Every two days I went to Paris for lunch and dinner at Mr. G.'s apartment until four or five in the morning. After that I went to Les Halles market to distribute my apples to wholesalers and agents. At first this life seemed very full and satisfying. However, at the beginning of October, I sensed what I had been unwilling to notice until then: Mr. G.'s health was becoming more and more precarious.

You know, Richard, I have already said that my superstitious naiveté made me blind. I believed that the death of Mr. G. would never occur. I saw his eternal presence, and when he improvised harmoniously on his little instrument — his eyes so radiant that the light, like a sacred substance, penetrated space and hearts — I could not imagine that it would end.

The last two months with him were of an extraordinary intensity. It grew with each lunch, each supper, always more and more moving. I compare this with what happens in the final stages of life for large old fruit trees, though I did not know about this phenomenon at the time. In the season before they die, the trees bear more fruit than ever — more fruit than leaves, and more beautiful than ever before. But the following spring they only show sad dead branches without any buds.

You will perhaps tell me, my dear Richard, that I have succumbed to the whirlwind of infatuation with Mr. G. and write only beautiful things while keeping silent about the bad ones and the more or less dark rumors that were widespread around him, both before and after his departure. My answer is simple.

First, I write only about what I have seen or felt.

Then I easily understand that other people whose masks were unceremoniously torn off displayed their wounds by spreading malicious, indecent rumors. The most famous example is obviously that of Katherine Mansfield, whom Mr. G. welcomed for a few weeks during the terminal phase of her life in a gesture of kindness for which he received only a splattering of muck in return.

Even in the groups, some people viewed him with distance or maintained a rather negative attitude toward him. I remember a lady who was a bit of a nymphomaniac whom he singled out one day, shedding some light on her relations with Cupid: "You well know the one with his bow decorated with many flowers who shoots an arrow in the center of the heart. In your case, Madame, and also in other biped creatures, the arrow must then be removed from the ass."

So too, money questions evoked the familiar negative stories. The sums necessary to feed so many people noon and evening, seven days a week, twelve months a year, did not fall from the sky, not to mention the food which he regularly offered to miserable Russian emigrants. He took from the rich to give to the poor and thereby engaged everyone. Isn't that reasonable and worthy of praise? Mr. G. often talked about this, making clear that he had to shear his sheep. "Only naive people can be content to say: Legendary Prince Mouchransky is giving away all his money."

I was never "shorn" myself, since he never asked me for money. But once at the beginning of October 1949, unexpectedly, I received quite a large sum from a wholesaler which was not listed in my accounts. I gave it to Mme. de S. to give to Mr. G.

Later at lunch, he said to me, mentioning the exact amount, "That, little thing. From you I need this: learn and live my ideas and principles, and then pass them on to others. *Sie! Deutscher*

Oberlokomotifconduktor! (You! Chief locomotive driver!)" In Germany every man is always an "ober" in charge of someone else or of something.

That same day Lise asked me to help her tidy up after everyone had left. This had nothing to do with the donation I had made for the first time. No particular intention was hidden behind it. It was simply that Mr. G. was becoming weaker and weaker, Lise did more and more work each day and she needed help. As busy as I was with this unfamiliar manual task of cleaning — strange, ambivalent and unrelated thoughts crossed my mind.

I saw the secret pride of those who give, especially those who give money, along with a particular form of self-esteem held by those who wash the dishes, a commonly despised job. Such contradictory situations shake the inevitable sense of one's social position, so much so that one no longer knows what or who one is, master or servant — if one is between the two or above the two, depending on one's mood and whether or not one is tired.

Only Mr. G. could judge whether a person was mature enough to change his or her "idiot." He alone decided and then he would organize a real party. I participated twice, once for a woman and once for a man. Changing "idiot," Mr. G. explained, required long hard work against one's own harmful tendencies, which allowed one to understand one's neighbor on a higher level.

Those who regularly came to his apartment already felt the need to change. They knew why they stayed late every evening before taking up their workload the next day at the office or elsewhere. I heard him say more than once before addressing one or another person to warn him that he would be better off going to the movies or to the theater: "No spectators here."

To place oneself in front of Mr. G. was to accept being put to the test constantly and to accept that some of one's previously ignored tendencies would be revealed. One evening for example — when, due to the crowd around the main table, I had taken my plate to a spot in the adjacent room — he called me back to inform me that someone had coughed in the next room and that an investigation was needed to find out who it was. Cunning actor, he looked at me sternly. There I was: standing stunned, blushing, embarrassed and uncomfortable. After a while, Mme. de S. compassionately rescued me: "Say it was you. It doesn't matter and in fact no one coughed."

Mr. G. himself added: "Stupid thing always wanting to defend yourself. Have you seen that now?"

Subsequently, I often noticed this trait — one of which, previously, I hadn't had the slightest idea. Mr. G. mentioned several times that each person has a chief feature, a specific dominant tendency which they tend to completely ignore. This topic generated endless discussions among us. Everyone obviously would have liked to know their chief feature — while continuing to hide it, of course.

One sunny spring day, an American student of a certain age offered Mr. G. a ride through Paris and the Bois de Boulogne in a horse-drawn carriage. A woman in the party told me later: "The American was squirming in his seat. One could sense from his agitation that an important question was burning in him. He absolutely had to speak to Mr. G., who paid no attention to him. As everyone knows, Mr. G. loves carriage rides and always accompanies them with the same humorous remarks, like: 'Sparrows, which usually have to be satisfied with the oil of cars, will at least have something to eat.'"

The American finally spat it out: *"Please Mr. Gurdjieff* tell me, if you please, my chief feature."

"It is obvious," replied Mr. G. "It is the one that makes you ask such a stupid question in such a beautiful moment."

Mr. G.'s regular bistro was at the corner of rue des Acacias and avenue Mac-Mahon. He usually arrived every day around ten o'clock and sat by habit at a table that was reserved for him. At that time we had tacit permission to sit near him and wait in silence for him to begin speaking. I went there several times while a few British and Americans were chatting and making small talk, often joined by the owner of the café.

In the last months of Mr. G's life, he would often return to sit in this bistro alone between four and six in the afternoon, watching the street, immobile and meditative. A few privileged people or members of his family sometimes settled next to him. I used to see him sitting there when I happened to be standing on the platform of the bus going up Mac-Mahon Avenue and I thought I detected his black eyes.

His sister, a very simple woman who was married to an Armenian, once told me: "I never understood what my brother does or has done, but what I understand is that I have never loved any human being as much as I love him. So I keep myself busy as much as possible cleaning his house. I do this better than the French."

His nephew, the son of this lady, bore a striking resemblance to him. I never spoke to him.

Mr. G. often received people with whom he spoke Russian and whom I sometimes saw with him in the street or in cafés. A gentleman of a certain age, quite elegant, his hair and mustache slicked black, sometimes sat very near to him at the table. His name was Mr. Gabo, and he seemed to be close to Mr. G. Late one evening when it was raining heavily, this gentleman asked me to take him home.

In front of his place, a beautiful flat a stone's throw from the Champs-Elysées, he invited me to come up and have a last glass of vodka. I accepted and asked him bluntly, while sipping my vodka, where and how he had known Mr. G. Quite frankly, he told me: "I was a young good-for-nothing police inspector in the Tsar's empire with a number of things on my conscience. Once I got Mr. G. out of a real bind in Moscow and probably saved his life. It was certainly the only good deed of my life at the time. He in turn probably saved my life. When I was wanted everywhere during the revolution he helped me get out of Russia and go abroad. But above all, I owe him a greater gratitude for having subsequently made of me an honest man. Of his teaching and his spirituality I understand nothing, but I know that without him, if I had not died, I would have been a completely fallen man."

Later, as I was going down the stairs, I wondered, "Will he also make of me a passably honest man?"

Perhaps I was expecting something different from Mr. Gabo.

Chapter XVI

THE LAST DAYS—THE DEATH OF MISTER GURDJIEFF

During September and October of 1949, when I was with Mr. G. in the steam baths, I saw his physical strength diminish week by week. His feet swelled — slightly at first then so badly that walking became painful. He drove his car himself for a while longer as if relieved to be sitting behind the wheel, steering his vehicle skillfully through Parisian traffic, though a little too fast for my liking. I sometimes sat to his right.

One evening as I was standing in the kitchen where the crowd had relegated me, I caught snippets of an astonishing conversation that was taking place in English around the table. It was about the relationship that one of the English visitors had with the royal household which sometimes invited him to London. Mr. G. quite liked being provoked, regardless of whether the questions were more or less welcome. Someone asked: "If the King of England expressed the desire, would Mr. G. agree to receive him?"

Such questions in the form of a challenge or provocation always created a certain suspense, an anxious pause. Either the provocateur found himself scratched with a claw in one of his vulnerable parts, or Mr. G. commented in a terse and unexpected manner on an aspect of the question, expanding it in such a way that one could fish for pearls.

"That's an impossible utopia," he replied. "If the King of England comes to my house, if he wants to benefit, he must bring his entire population. But you, you are not bird droppings; you are a student of George Ivanovitch Gurdjieff. My rule, the rule that I teach: If you want to rise inwardly and avoid unnecessary complications, always stay very far from any man of power."

He often said that corruption, dirty dealings and cheating are mixed up in politics. One day someone who was uncomfortable with this viewpoint asked him: "But sir, aren't there also honest politicians?"

"Yes, of course there are," he replied, "but they end up serving as screens for the usual scoundrels and career-makers who use them and then reject and abandon them."

There was, in my opinion, a rare exception that Mr. G. could not have known about, since it occurred chiefly after his death. It is General de Gaulle, who after a long political career full of perilous adventures, left no fortune to his heirs. His family home, *La Boisserie*, where he died became a place of historical importance. It had to be sold shortly afterward by his family, who did not have the means to maintain it. Thus, there are valid reasons for considering de Gaulle an extraordinary anomaly in the political world. I am only confirming the words of Mr. G. and the exception that proves the rule.

By the end of September, Mr. G. became incapable of preparing meals by himself and organizing his house with the sole help of Lise to make it welcoming to so many people. Several women taking turns placed themselves at his disposal. Never, except at the very end, was a meal canceled.

One day Lise whispered in my ear: "He has great difficulty lifting his feet to get into the car. He said to me in an ironic tone, 'I would give them a thousand francs each time to help me.' Help him when you go to the hammam with him, especially on the way back."

On the next occasion — the next-to-last time we went to the steam bath — we took my car. I helped Mr. G. the best I could and he rewarded me with a grateful look. While bathing, his red and swollen feet, along with other signs of his sickly condition, were painful to witness, yet he did not seem to alter his behavior or mood. I did not feel that he was so ill. Or was it that I did not want to see?

I took him once again to the Russian pastry shop where he bought many things, although since he was walking with difficulty, he did not carry anything. The worried faces that welcomed us into his home convinced me that I had been too optimistic about his health. The meal was tense. He only ate a few small green onions sprinkled with herbs.

New guests often made the understandable mistake that Mr. G., expert in the preparation of these rich feasts, enjoyed the pleasures of the table himself and particularly liked to indulge. However, even though he emptied his glass with each toast, he ate very little.

The following week, around October 24, Mr. G. insisted again on going to the hammam, against the advice of several people and some cautious attempts to prevent him. His breathing was short. His eyes, feet, and legs were very swollen and blood vessels were protruding from his chest. He tried, barely succeeding, to recreate the joyfully masculine atmosphere that usually brought us together. When we returned to his building we had to carry him out of the car and into the elevator. Until now I had never seen him use the elevator to get to the first floor. None of us were allowed inside the apartment. We were told that he needed to rest.

More and more worried, I paced the surrounding streets for the next two hours. Then, no longer able to stand it, I went back and rang his doorbell, contrite and embarrassed. Marthe opened the door. With her angry snake-like gaze, she hissed venomous reproaches at me: "Really Grunwald, you are going too far."

Then Michel de S. appeared and calmly asked what brought me.

"I am very worried about the state of Mr. G.," I replied. "Earlier, I brought him home from the hammam. I have to go back to Chinon, and I would like to see him one more time."

In a generous gesture, Michel let me in, with a word of consolation to the exasperated Marthe: "One more, it doesn't matter much."

Mr. G., sitting on his little sofa in front of the table was speaking loudly and angrily in Russian more to himself, it seemed to me, than to anyone else. A few people were seated around him, concern and embarrassment evident on their faces. I found a seat, gradually becoming aware of a solemn calm beneath his enraged words — a beneficial appeasement, a gentle tenderness, like a spiritual incense that Mr. G. had furiously shaken from its container. I looked at Michel, who was smiling at me. Did he feel the same way? Mme. de S. also radiated a deep and peaceful serenity, unlike the others, whose tight expressions betrayed their fear and anxiety. The prepared dishes covered the table. I did not touch anything.

After some time I got up and stood in the doorway for a while. Mr. G. gave me a long look, his last blessing. I bowed in a deep salute and went to get my coat. Michel joined me in the entrance: "It is good that you came," he told me.

I returned directly via Chartres to Chinon, calm and serene. Driving slowly, more slowly than ever, I did not arrive at the estate until nightfall.

A few days later, around five in the afternoon on October 29, Nadia called to tell me: "Mr. G. died between ten-thirty and eleven o'clock this morning at the American hospital in Neuilly."

Frozen, phone in hand, I remained silent, aware of the first thoughts that arose in me. *How could you let this superstition about Mr. G.'s bodily immortality take root?* I reproached myself: *You tell yourself so many stories! And yet you could see that he was getting worse and worse!*

I was petrified, unable to respond to Nadia, who was still speaking. I felt duped, mystified, almost cheated. Really, he could not disappear like that, simply disappear!

Ten years later I understood my state at that moment, recognizing it as a characteristic example of a sudden collision between the surface consciousness and a deeper consciousness. I clearly understood that these thoughts rising from the depths about the immortality of Mr. G. did not concern his physical person but something of a completely different nature. I was interpreting the conviction that was growing within me and attributing it to his physical person. Still, my original naiveté was based on a fair apprehension of his spiritual person — that is to say, of his life's work, his share of immortality.

When I finally put the phone down I had no feeling of sadness. I accepted the obvious. It seemed suddenly as if I had gained a higher perspective, while being serenely present.

I rushed to the capital with my wife after quickly placing the children in safe hands. We drove silently toward Neuilly.

Many people were already gathered in the hospital courtyard. We entered the Chapel of Rest through a small garden. Mr. G. was lying on a platform about a meter from the ground surrounded by flowers, his beautiful swarthy face relaxed and still expressive despite his closed eyes. He was dressed in a dark suit with a white shirt and tie. I had never seen him like that. People known and unknown to me occupied the chairs arranged around him, quiet and still.

The rapidly-growing crowd required some organization. Each person who arrived was permitted to stay near Mr. G. for five minutes. Then small assemblies of around twenty people who knew each other from working in the same group took turns, standing watch for three or four hours, day and night, as much as possible.

In the hallway, where new people were constantly flocking, I met Lise at last, who told me about his final days. She explained that after I left the apartment, Mme. de S. called for three renowned doctors, but Mr. G. did not allow himself to be examined. "Give them their fees, but they leave me alone," he kept saying.

Finally, after discussions and entreaties, he gave in and submitted to a brief examination but stubbornly refused to leave his apartment, as the doctors demanded. However, Mme. de S. had already called America for a student and friend, Dr. Welch from New York. He arrived the next day and Mr. G. happily allowed himself to be transported to the American hospital where Dr. Welch could take care of him.

As Mr. G. was leaving the apartment, already lying on the ambulance stretcher, he called for his sister and gave her one last order, in a firm tone: "During my absence, nothing must be changed here." This brief command gave rise to many discussions among us afterward.

Mme. de S. and Lise accompanied Mr. G. to the hospital and never left him. "He was perfectly conscious the whole time," Lise added. "He spoke kindly to us. Dr. Welch looked after him with great attention. He punctured Mr. G.'s swollen abdomen and removed several liters of fluid. Mr. G. was very relieved and joked with us again. As recently as this morning, I didn't have the slightest impression that he was getting worse. Around ten thirty he called us, Mme. de S. and me, near his bed. He smiled at us, gave us a little wave and closed his eyes. The next moment, he was no longer breathing. He left gently, as if falling asleep. Next January he would have been seventy-three."

Back in the chapel, several girls were crying as they sat on the floor behind his body. One of them, her hair in disarray, let her tears flow abundantly though she remained without moving. Among those standing watch over him, however, no one sobbed. Mr. G. remained thus exposed for six days, allowing his students and disciples to come from all over the world. In those days it took almost twenty-four hours to get to Paris from the United States.

After helping a friend who had come from Savoie with his family by towing his broken-down car to a garage, Denise and I spent the night at her parents' home. We returned to the chapel the following day. To her regret, Denise needed to leave soon afterward, so I accompanied her to the train station.

On the evening of the second day our group, led by Mme. H., had its turn keeping vigil near Mr. G.'s remains, which were immersed in a sea of flowers. I will never forget Mme. H.'s face as she sat near his head, surrounded by all of us. I had been dozing for a few moments. When I looked up I saw her attentive and transfigured expression and how her face had taken on a singular beauty.

I spent the next five days at the hospital, in the hall or the chapel, available for multiple errands — getting flowers for example, or making trips to the train stations or Le Bourget airport to pick up people arriving from far away. Many conversations took place on these rides, always fraternal and often enriching, with people who had been students of Mr. G. for a long time.

On one of these evenings Tchekhovitch, an old and strong Russian to whom Mr. G. regularly gave real tongue-lashings — incomprehensible to me, but in a tone that left no doubt about the nature of his words — told me his story: "In Russia I was a professional wrestler. It was the only thing I knew how to do, so I was still earning my keep as a wrestler when I met G. I. G. in Constantinople. He and his wife literally charmed me. They fascinated me so much that I wanted them to take me into their service immediately. But I was so clumsy that he whose manual skills were so astonishing often had to redo my work. However, clumsy as I was, I never stopped boasting of my strength as a wrestler and I flexed my muscles for people to admire."

"One day Mr. G. said to me: 'You brag about your strength, but a donkey has much more than you. As you are now, you are not even as good as a donkey. As for your head, we can really compare it to that of a donkey. You must develop your mind, twisted monster that you are.' It's a Russian expression that I don't know how to translate.

"Then he continued: 'You must become a real man. There will always be animals stronger than you.'

"From that moment on I started reading. I tried to acquire knowledge. I became his student, and I still am today. He told me off at least once a week, a real correction. I don't really know, but I think I always liked that he took care of me like that. In some ways I remained an oaf, but an honest oaf."

Upon receiving the news, students from California, Texas, South America, came to Paris as quickly as possible. Intimate exchanges continued day and night between people who did not know each other or barely knew each other, animated and connected by the same atmosphere of inner solidarity. This crowd that was assembled at the hospital obviously attracted attention and curiosity. We managed, I think, to keep the journalists and other curious people away and firmly turned away the strangers. It was only after the funeral that most newspapers published obituaries. Andrieux, a member of the group and a press photographer, took a number of photos of Mr. G.'s remains.

November was beginning. All Saints' Day was frosty and the Day of the Dead even colder, but early in the afternoon of November 5th, the day the body was put in the coffin, the sun shone. I had arrived very early and was standing in the chapel when I saw a few tears streaming down the beautiful face of Mme. de S., who never lost her clear serenity. "Tears of human emotion," she said later. Six men — four of Mr. G.'s Russian friends, a Frenchman and Michel de S. — carried the coffin into the mortuary van and placed it in front on the right.

In the Orthodox cathedral on rue Daru, flowers and wreaths without any inscription covered the catafalque. A gigantic cross of red roses, very beautiful, two to three meters high, made an extraordinary impression.

The Metropolitan head of the Russian Orthodox church in Paris, an old man wearing a high round headdress, led the solemn ceremony surrounded by several priests with long beards. The extraordinarily deep bass voice of an elderly singer filled the entire cathedral with its powerful vibrations all the way up to the dome and penetrated our bodies and hearts. I have never heard another man's voice of this quality: deep, pure, and beautiful, capable of making all those who heard it shudder in a sacred rapture. The Russian mixed choirs also gave forth this intense beauty. These songs are repeated every year during the anniversary ceremony.

A candle was given to each participant and the flame from the altar was transmitted one by one until the entire space of the cathedral was illuminated. The light shone on each face and spread in moving waves like a luminous sea. Finally, the bishop circled the coffin three times swinging the silver chains of his censer, releasing the fragrant fumes.

The long funeral procession headed towards rue des Colonels Renard, where it stopped for a moment, and slowly moved through the narrow streets of the neighborhood greeted by a crowd of people watching from windows and stores.

I managed to keep my car behind the funeral van as we drove

at high speed toward Fontainebleau. Most of the vehicles got separated, especially those of foreigners. It was not so easy to reach Fontainebleau at the time. The highway did not exist and the journey to the cemetery through the forest took more than two hours. Mme. H., seated to my right, remained silent. Behind me Mrs. March was speaking to Jacqueline about Mr. G.

The sun had long since disappeared. A fine, dense rain was falling, freezing and turning the ground of the cemetery into mud. Mrs. March showed us the graves of Mr. G.'s mother and wife. Unlike the other graves, which were made from blocks of cut marble, theirs were made from a large surface of green grass surrounded by a small wall and a border of flowers. At each end approximately six meters apart, two tall, slender, irregular stones faced each other, marking the precise location of the tombs. Next to the grave of Mr. G.'s wife, a freshly dug grave on the lawn awaited his coffin; on the other side, a large dark green cypress sheltered a stone bench.

"He sometimes meditated sitting on this bench," explained Mrs. March, "at the time of the Prieuré in the thirties." Then she added: "I then had the impression that the two slender stones of his mother and his wife were leaning noticeably towards each other."

The coffin — carried by the same six men and followed by the assembly of calm and disciplined mourners — was placed in the open grave. Only Andrieux the photographer wandered between one and the other to fulfill his duties. I climbed onto the small ledge of Katherine Mansfield's grave to watch the ceremony. An orthodox priest with a gigantic black beard led the burial assisted by two young acolytes. He sang for a long time in Russian and spread the smoke of incense widely. For more than twenty years this same priest led the anniversary ceremonies at Mr. G.'s tomb. Over the years he sang more and more faintly, his voice trembled and he walked with increasing difficulty. We saw his beard, while remaining still gigantic, change from black on the day of the funeral, through all shades of gray to a magnificent white.

The officiants withdrew, leaving us in a large semi-circle

around the open grave. The fine, heavy rain did not stop. Mme. de S., all in black, advanced alone. In the most serious and striking moment of the day, with a dignified and solemn gesture, she knelt in the mud and bowed before the buried coffin, her head to the ground. Then she tossed a few flowers and a small shovelful of earth on the coffin in a final tribute that each of us repeated.

I remained for a long time in front of the open grave overcome by a completely new and pleasant sensitivity, touched by sweet feelings as the thought came to me: I did not know either of my two grandfathers; they died before I was born. Mr. G. is actually not my teacher, since — apart from a few brief interviews and certain personal and striking remarks and unlike many of the people here — he did not teach me directly. However, I spent hours near him and in me there arises for him the reflection of a child's love.

Spontaneously and without any presumption, I identified with his "grandson" in spirit. Was he not really my spiritual grandfather? Wasn't I in fact much closer to Hassein, Beelzebub's grandson, than to anyone else? This is still how I feel. *If, dear grandfather, you see me from above, I hope not to disappoint you.*

This, my dear Richard, is where my story ends. Events had raised me, in a crescendo, to a peak from which I contemplated a wonderful landscape. It was necessary to go back, simultaneously free and constrained, down into the valley.

It is now up to you, Richard, to gauge and judge whether I have succeeded throughout these pages in describing this crescendo and whether this account, as close as possible to the lived truth, can be useful to our brothers and sisters.

Chapter XVII
TOWARD SOMETHING ELSE—EXILE IS ALSO A MOURNING

In the following months, I had no rest. We carefully sorted the apple harvest which had been stored in fruit cellars near Paris and I supervised its gradual sale at the Les Halles market. A politically influential family from Sologne bought the Vaugaudry estate in 1950 after its castle, land, houses, outbuildings, agricultural machines and tools had been examined and evaluated many times. When I returned to Vaugaudry ten years later, the orchards had been renewed, large cold storage rooms installed, artificial ponds dug for irrigation and the roofs repaired. The owner of the place, a retired doctor, expressed his gratitude to me for having recommended Mr. Lavenne, who now managed the estate and also assumed the functions of first deputy mayor of Chinon.

My family and I settled in the Parisian suburbs, in a spacious house with a beautiful garden, not far from the homes of Mme. H. and two friends from the group and near schools for our children. We were also close to a train station which made it possible to reach the center of Paris in forty minutes. Our weekly groups, in which my wife also participated, were now held in Mr. G.'s apartment and on Saturday evenings; our Movements class took place in Salle Pleyel.

In the fall of 1950 I took the scientific exams in physics, chemistry and biology, a necessary step before beginning medical school. I studied intensely, but the difficulties of our new situation weighed on my time, and I decided to overcome the sclerosis of my intellectual apparatus with more regular and practical work. I thus took on a job as an apprentice potter with a friend, the director of a ceramics workshop, and familiarized myself with this art while devoting two hours of intense work to medicine every day. In June 1951, already very experienced in pottery and almost a ceramist, I successfully passed the first exams at the Paris medical faculty.

Six and a half years of concentration on learning followed, along with daily work at the hospital. I stayed up late at night over my books, devoting my Saturdays and Sundays to them as well. At the beginning, a sustained effort was required, but little by little I became more comfortable. Never failing any exam, I finally became a doctor in 1957 — with more theoretical than practical knowledge, along with specialized training and good experience in psychiatry.

By a strange symmetry, leaving my studies was as difficult as entering them. I was already seeing patients, even though I continued to study at night and acquire new qualifications at the Faculty of Science, in psychophysiology, for example. Many masters taught me, some real authorities in their field, such as: Professors Heuer, Henri Baruk, Gilbert Dreyfus and also Doctor Salmanoff, Robert Desoille and Paul Diel, the Viennese psychologist living in Paris, not to mention Professor Pierre Aboulker and Jean Vaysse, about whom I have already spoken — and others to whom I owe a great deal.

My inner work consisted of patiently putting into practice the information I had previously collected with emotional enthusiasm, though other directions were emerging at the same time. I followed the lessons and exercises proposed by my instructors, Mme. de S. and Henri T., who encouraged us to work methodically and regularly. My studies helped me as the method, regularity and my personal initiative developed in parallel. The Movements classes took on more and more importance, and later Mme. de S. preserved this part of the work in films.

I rarely did the Movements, however, due to a lack of aptitude for harmonious dance gestures and a lack of time.

My financial comfort was a thing of the past, my capital

— that is, the apple money — having to last until I was established as a doctor. I scrupulously respected the rule stated by Mr. G.: to give nine percent of one's earnings for one's spiritual instruction. Mme. de S., who never asked me for anything, was therefore surprised when I asked her to accept nine percent of this capital. I insisted. I knew the financial difficulties of the teaching and that this money would be welcome, but above all I would have despised myself if I had not fulfilled such an obvious rule. It appeared to me and it still does, even today, to be comparable to the animal sacrifices in the temples of ancient times. Donors offered part of their herds as capital. A sacrifice without which nothing can be acquired is the link.

Other premises were emerging. Which ones, will you ask me? Mr. G had sown in me a certain quality of initiative whose growth and eventual harvest gradually made themselves known. I admired and esteemed Mme. de S. then, as today. I was her student and I am grateful to her, for her teaching and for her way of being, so dignified and appropriate in every situation. Yet what was germinating in me under the impulse of Mr. G took a noticeably different direction, and did not always accord with the generally prevailing *bon ton*.

I opened my medical office on rue Dombasle in the 15th arrondissement from 1957 to 1959 and then on rue de Rennes in Montparnasse, where you met me shortly afterward in 1961, my dear Richard. The rest of the story you know for yourself for the most part.

The year 1949 was a pivotal year, casting into shadow the events that seemed important to me before then, which I have recounted: adolescence in Vienna, exile, war and return from war.[1] I now understand that I was already in exile in Vienna as a youth — an inner exile, which the outer exile exacerbated ultimately for the better.

Because grace allowed me to meet Ludolf Schild and

---

[1] François Grunwald wrote his memoir as a three-part manuscript of which this is the third part. The first part covers his adolescence and exile, and the second part — his experiences in WWII. The full memoir is available in French, under the title *Un chemin hors de l'exil: De Freud à Gurdjieff*.

become his close friend, and then through Ludolf meet George Ivanovitch Gurdjieff, who set me on the difficult path leading toward myself out of human exile. Since I am no longer completely in exile and know where my home port lies, the details of my life are no longer so important.

Persistent work — a persevering struggle against inertia, indifference and negativity — is always the prerequisite for emerging from exile, toward a home, a true homeland. I have experienced this journey back to my true homeland and although my journey may be in its infancy, I have an unalterable taste for it. Strength to achieve this aim is given to those who have the indubitable conviction that this homeland so ardently desired can really be reached and who know in practice that inertia is exile. These two men whose memory fills me with gratitude awakened in me a firm and indestructible confidence. I would like to end my story with the wonderful verses of Lynceus, the watchman of the tower from Goethe's second *Faust*:

> *Ihre glücklichen Augen*
> *Was je ihr gesehn,*
> *Es sei, wie es wolle,*
> *Es war doch so schön!*

> O my fortunate eyes,
> Everything you saw,
> Come what will,
> It was so beautiful!

Yet I cannot repeat these beautiful and simple verses. The murders of my mother and my sister in Auschwitz do not allow it. Any lived event may be transformed by "fortunate eyes" into a valid and sometimes ultimately beautiful experience, but their murders were not events I experienced. They took place somewhere far away in secret, in the infernal depths of darkness, a frightening absence of memory that is akin to exile.

Exile is also mourning, the loss of one's spiritual homeland, nostalgia for home, which is always somehow inhabited by one's mother. This is where the connection is made.

Completed on September 28, 1987, early in the morning.
Translation from German to French, summer 1990.

Francine Grunwald

AFTERWORD

On December 24, 2015, I took the train to Bellegarde to join my husband at his parents' house for Christmas Eve.

There was a couple in front of me in the train compartment, the lady giving foie gras sandwiches to the man, and we started a conversation. The man told me he had a spiritual publishing house. When I mentioned that I was leaving for India in a week, he asked who had first introduced me to India. I answered that it was my father, and he asked what my father's name was. I told him, "François Grunwald."

He answered, "I know him very well! He is a friend! I have been trying to contact your sister Marie-Claude for years to get photos of your father."

His name was Charles Antoni. On the train platform in Bellegarde we exchanged our phone numbers, and we met again when I returned from my trip to India. I gave him the manuscript of my father's memoirs. Two days later, he told me that he would like to publish it. I asked my brother and sister for their agreement and the project took shape with Charles Antoni's enthusiasm.

He considered François Grunwald as his Spiritual Father. They had met on the way to India, each going there for the first time to meet a Master or Guru — Su padma menon for François Grunwald, and for Charles, a yogi living in a forest.

My father studied medicine, specializing in psychiatry. He organized a Gurdjieff group in Stuttgart, Germany, where he taught for several years.

He missed a living master. One day when he was giving a

lecture in Paris on "The outcome of an analysis = spiritual path, otherwise neurosis," he was booed. But at the exit, someone was waiting and invited him to meet an Indian master who was visiting Paris. Then began another spiritual adventure for him, and he went to India to follow his teachings. There, he also met his second wife, Odile. He often went to Kerala, making long stays there with his Guru.

He became a great psychiatrist, working in collaboration with Viktor Frankl in Vienna, Madame Dolto in France, etc. He separated from his wife Denise. His second wife, Odile, died young. He returned to Denise and remarried her, with their four children as wedding witnesses. He died surrounded by his family, in love and peace.

His memoirs were commissioned by a German publisher, but as the manuscript was too long, the publisher wanted to cut a lot of it. He refused, saying that he was writing for his children, so that they would know their father's story.

Thank you, Father. See you soon.

Mr. Gurdjieff said, "Parents make a hole in the sky."

www.ingramcontent.com/pod-product-compliance
Lightning Source LLC
Chambersburg PA
CBHW030140170426
43199CB00008B/139